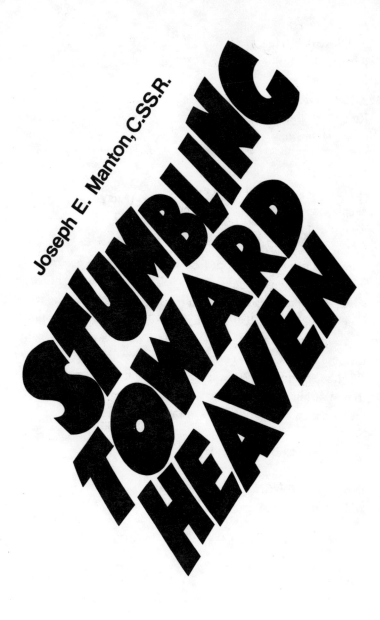

Joseph E. Manton, C.SS.R.

STUMBLING TOWARD HEAVEN

Our Sunday Visitor, Inc.
Huntington, Indiana 46750

Imprimi Potest:
Rev. Joseph Hurley, C.SS.R.
Provincial

Nihil Obstat:
Rev. Msgr. John G. Hogan
Censor Librorum

Imprimatur:
✠Humberto Cardinal Medeiros
Archbishop of Boston
August 1, 1978

Some chapters in this work first appeared in the *Liguorian*, Liguori Publications, Liguori, Missouri, and have been quoted in whole or in part. Most scriptural texts contained herein are taken from *The Jerusalem Bible*, copyright © 1966 by Darton, Longman & Todd, Ltd., London, England, and Doubleday & Company, Inc., New York, New York, as well as from the *New American Bible*, copyright © 1970 by the Confraternity of Christian Doctrine, Washington, D.C. The author and publisher are grateful to the aforementioned for the use of their material.

ISBN: 0-87973-626-7
Library of Congress Catalog Card Number: 78-71262

Cover Design by James E. McIlrath

Published, printed and bound
in the United States of America

626

contents

gallery of halos

The Making of a Saint

June 19, 1977 is a significant date for Catholics the world over, but especially for those in the United States. The date marks the canonization of America's first male citizen: John Nepomucene Neumann.

Overnight Saint John Neumann pole-vaults into international prominence. But how did he become an official saint? Suddenly he stands front and center in the spotlight. But what has been happening all this time backstage?

To one just learning English, the word "canonize" probably sounds like the roar of artillery. Originally it meant that on the day one was declared a saint, his or her name was put, for that day only, in the canon of the Mass. But forever after, that person is in the official catalog of *Who's Who in Heaven*.

Sainthood is a towering honor. It is no small distinction for a Nobel prizewinner to bow from the waist, accept the scroll and fold the check. It is not a minor accolade to stand upon the stadium's central block and feel the gold medal of an Olympic champion looped around one's perspiring neck. But to be enrolled in the bright band of canonized saints is a radiant glory that soars beyond all these. It constitutes membership in the world's most exclusive club. To have one's heroic-size portrait unveiled in St. Peter's while silver trumpets blare and church bells tumble wildly in their towers and thousands upon thousands burst into exultant song — this is the rarest and grandest honor of all.

Canonization is, to be sure, an exclusively Catholic procedure. Protestants are willing to name their children after saints, like Francis and Bernard and George, but they do not acknowledge the conferring of a contemporary halo. Not that they scowl at the notion of moderns who have attained extraordinary holiness; they just do not officially recognize such an achievement.

To a Catholic, however, sainthood is an ongoing phenomenon. Any age of history, from the apostolic to the atomic, can produce outstanding pioneers of piety and mighty monarchs in the kingdom of self-control. Such extraordinary spirits the Catholic not only canonizes, but to these selfless souls — poor in this world's goods, chaste in a burning body and steadfastly walking in the path of duty — the Catholic also addresses his prayers. The logic is simple. He argues that such a man served God so well that God must love him dearly, and will listen to him if he pleads the cause of others. From the clean hands of a spotless saint the Lord will more willingly receive a request than from hands smudged with too many sins.

But, while the Catholic Church recognizes saints and warmly welcomes newcomers into their exalted ranks, the last thing that it desires is a swarming multiplication of their number. Piety has always cherished the devout conviction that the day on which the saint leaves this earth by the pedestrian route of death is the glorious occasion of his birthday in heaven. In this narrow liturgical sense the Church actually favors birth control. The Church does not want a flood of new saints. The gate to canonization is narrow and must be kept so. The sublime title of saint must never become cheap.

Precisely to prevent overkill, the Church has arranged a rugged obstacle race that any candidate must survive before he reaches the coveted halo. (Need it be said here that it is the candidate's dedicated supporters who are determined that he pass the test? The man himself, if he truly is holy, could not care less. He already has it made.)

For many centuries there was no legal process. Many a saint became such merely by acclamation. The people among whom he lived were convinced of his extraordinary holiness and they carried him into heaven, as it were, on the eager shoulders of local enthusiasm.

Then Pope Benedict XIV (1740-1758) changed all the rules of the game. He pushed back the fences, traced out the clear foul lines, and appointed official scorekeepers. Since then the requirements for canonization have become so rigid that during the last few centuries out of millions of Catholics only about one a year has made the Church's Hall of Fame.

Canonization usually begins with a small reputation, as the Mississippi begins with a bubbling brook in the backwoods of Minnesota. Harry Holy impresses those around him as a man of extraordinary virtue. When he dies, the whisper goes about, long after his wake, "He was a living saint!" The local bishop reluctantly listens. (In these matters priests are predictably skeptical and bishops almost professionally cynical.)

But in the rare case, conviction persists, pious pressure insists and an official investigation is opened. Witnesses present testimony. Objections are raised and answered. The subject's life, his words, his deeds, his writings — all are stared at under the microscope, and studied for faults or flaws.

At long last, and it could take years, these local ecclesiastical examiners are convinced that Harry Holy did live a truly saintly life. The facts are so impressive and the evidence so persuasive that the bishops of Harry's country feel bound to send the case on to Rome for further investigation. Harry is now labeled a "servant of God," not exactly a lofty title considering what he has been through.

Next, all the local testimony rides on a conveyor belt to the proper Roman congregation, that is, the official Vatican committee charged with a further and far deeper scrutiny of the facts. This congregation numbers about twenty-five cardinals and as many clergy assistants. Usually there are hundreds of "causes," as the proposals for canonization are called, either sleeping in dusty pigeonholes or poised on the launching pad, depending on the energy or the apathy of the proponents.

In recent times most new saints have been members of a religious order. Obviously any process that may take fifty years or more has to have behind it a continuing organization to foster the cause, and the regrettable but grimly necessary funds to finance it. That influence plays no part is wholesomely evident in the fact that in the last four hundred years only two popes have been raised to the honors of the altar, though many undoubtedly holy men have sat in the Chair of Peter.

The sieve for ultimate approval is exceptionally fine. Of candidates proposed only about five percent make it. For its own protection the Church moves in these matters with all the headlong enthusiasm of an arthritic glacier. The first slow Roman step is to examine the servant of God's life all over again, reviewing the testimony, questioning the motives, fluoroscoping for flaws of character.

Enter here the notorious devil's advocate. He is a priest or prelate whose sworn duty it is to be the promoter of the faith, that is, the grim guardian of the gate to sainthood. Most people visualize this devil's advocate as the crusty combination of a vinegary Scrooge and a dyspeptic district attorney. In real life he may more closely resemble a jovial Friar Tuck. But no matter what his personal architecture or natural temperament may be, the devil's advocate has taken a solemn oath to let no unworthy person pass.

Well, suppose all the hurdles have been cleared, and the candidate does pass. Suppose his life has been adjudged irreproachable and his virtue heroic. In that event he is accorded the title of "venerable." This means that the Church has every prudent reason to believe that the man in question may be in heaven.

But now there must come corroboration from on high. This has to evidence itself in the form of four unquestionable miracles. Should the candidate be a martyr, two of these miracles can be waived. In the case of a non-martyr, there have been rare instances, where for weighty reasons, fewer miracles have been accepted as sufficient.

Two conditions must be met by the miracles: (1) They must have taken place after the saint's death, and (2) they must have been obtained through prayers to the saint. Usually the miracle is an incredible cure, a breathtaking recovery. It would be framing the obvious with neon lights to observe that here the Church has to be grimly wary and coldly suspicious rather than sentimentally naive. Too much is at stake.

In practice, at this point the Church wisely steps back and leaves the examination of the evidence and the medical decision to those in the medical profession. The ultimate judgment, to be sure, is the Church's; but only in those cases where there is ironclad proof of both an irreversible condition and an inexplicable cure is the Church even remotely interested. In fact, volumes of so-called "cures" that would make the average reader's eyes bulge, gather dust in forgotten file cabinets that bear the sober label "rejected."

No court in the world is so strict in its investigations and hearings as that which determines sainthood. Halos, like diamonds, cannot be allowed to become common. And the Church just cannot afford to be wrong.

At any rate, once two undoubted miracles have been established, the candidate for sainthood moves from the level plain of "venerable" to the higher plateau of "blessed." With the second two miracles he rises to the mountain peak where he can plant the supreme banner of "saint."

On second thought, not really he — not the man under consideration. If he is really the saint he has been made out to be, he would back away from the whole project. No one would protest more sincerely the time, the trouble, the cost entailed in the long, rigorous, expensive process of the making of a saint. But, on the other hand, unless there is some kind of standard and some sort of selection board, how could we ever know our contemporary heroes and heroines of holiness? How could we ever be sure that what Christ founded on Peter is still the *holy* Catholic Church? It is reassuring to hear the answer ring out from time to time in the silver trumpets of St. Peter's and the canonization of a new saint.

Numero Uno

If the land has its changing seasons that run from green spring to flowery summer to bronzed autumn and white winter, the Church too has its varying climates and shifting moods.

On Ash Wednesday we gather before the altar in gray repentance, on All Souls' Day in black bereavement, on red-and-green Christmas and white-and-gold Easter in glorious joy. But the canonization of a saint, especially for his brethren in that particular religious order, is a day of triumph and of gratitude. For them it is a special family celebration because one of their own has made it to the top!

The Redemptorists are not a prominent group, like the Jesuits or the Benedictines, the Dominicans or the Franciscans. Perhaps that is why they are all the prouder (in a humble way, of course) that the first male U.S. citizen to be canonized came from their ranks. He died as the fourth bishop of Philadelphia; but before he was a bishop he was a Redemptorist. In fact he was the first vocation that the order attracted in the United States.

It was in January 1842 that John Neumann laid his trembling hand on the Holy Book and took his sacred vows. Since then, hundreds of young men have followed him. Today it is a warm feeling to look back and remember that the very first signature in that long list, our Abou Ben Adhem, who leads all the rest, is John Nepomucene Neumann, and before his name we can write *Saint*!

Like Saint Alphonsus, the founder of the Redemptorists, John Neumann was a secular priest prior to becoming a Redemptorist. But priest or not, every candidate is first supposed to make a novitiate, a strict year of silence and prayer and preparation, under the direction of a novice master. Father Neumann's novice master was a missionary who was more often than not, away preaching missions. So, the novice had to be his own novice master, and in a sense (one that might make a contortionist envious), sit at his own feet and listen to his own lectures. Fortunately, the future proved that he did not need a novice master. To make young Father Neumann a novice in the ordinary sense would have been like setting a skilled surgeon to rolling bandages, or a concert pianist to playing the scales.

Just two years later, Father Neumann was made the rector of the newly formed Redemptorist community in Pittsburgh. With him were two other Redemptorists, a Father Seelos and a Father Mueller. They had three cots with a couple of sheets hung between them for privacy. Since then, Father Seelos has been nominated for canonization, and has been officially declared Venerable.

I do not wish to be facetious or frothy, but I cannot help recalling that the salty legend persists among Redemptorists that the real saint was the man who managed to live between the two technical saints. One of the holiest men I ever knew (Father Francis Kenzel, the Redemptorist who wrote the famed "Pilate's Daughter"), used to love to quote, and I can still hear him:

> *To live with the saints above,*
> *Ah, that's eternal glory.*
> *But to live with the saints on earth —*
> *Ah, that's another story!*

I bring this out in order to point out that the saints are different. Like the rich, they are not like us. A saint is an unusual person. Saint John Neumann, for example, was not an outgoing, gregarious, sociable, affable, genial character. He was more often silent than speaking. When he spoke, it was in a low voice with a marked accent. When he slept, it was often not in a bed but in a chair. When he collapsed in death on a snowy Philadelphia street, he had a chain of sharp hooks piercing his flesh.

So do not get the idea that the saints are like the rest of us. This is why there are so few of them canonized. John Neumann had taken a vow (like Saint Alphonsus) never to lose a moment of time. Such a man was not likely to be leisurely and relaxed and open to easy and idle conversation. To be honest, he inspired not affection but awe.

Perhaps it was this driving dedication that made the Roman authorities choose him to be the head of all Redemptorists in the United States when he was only thirty-five years old. Father Neumann held the helm for two years. He never wanted it and there were some Redemptorists who did not want him. The issue was expansion. Father Neumann felt that since the Redemptorists had been established in the United States only a dozen years, the program should be to consolidate the existing Redemptorist foundations rather than risk ruin by spreading the few men too thinly.

Still, the humble Father Neumann felt he might easily be wrong. So he humbly offered his resignation. No longer Redemptorist provincial, he became rector of St. Alphonsus in Baltimore. Well, if the Redemptorists did not want him to be provincial, the Church ironically wanted him to hold the higher post of bishop. The archbishop of Baltimore had hinted often enough, but that March afternoon when Father Neumann came back from a sick call and saw a bishop's ring and pectoral cross gleaming on the bare table in his little room, he knew too well. In vain, he appealed to Rome; the Pope overruled all his objections.

They called him "the little bishop" because he was only five feet two inches tall; and on his graying brown hair the miter soared up like a steeple on a tiny chapel. But he was little only in size.

Measure his accomplishments and he towered up like an Alp. In his eight short episcopal years, he saw to the building of eighty new churches and thirty-five new schools. He founded one group of Sisters, still flourishing, and rescued another from perishing. He introduced into America the Forty Hours on a diocesan level, and wrote a catechism that was used long after his death.

Bishop or not, John Neumann was still a Redemptorist. He had chosen as his coat of arms, the seal of the congregation. When some Redemptorists said he was now an outsider, he appealed to the Pope and received reassurance that he was still a Redemptorist.

Every week Bishop Neumann walked across Philadelphia streets to confession in the Redemptorist church of St. Peter's. Every month, he went there for his day of recollection. Every year, he lived there for his ten days' retreat. While he was there, off came his episcopal red, and on went the simple habit of Saint Alphonsus. After each meal he slipped into the kitchen to help the Brothers wash the dishes. Here was a truly humble man after the meek and humble heart of Christ!

The Church has seen in its long centuries all kinds of saints. Some have been long and thin like window poles; some have been short and squat like hassocks. Some have been virgins, some martyrs, some cardinals, some kings. But among them all, at the moment, Bishop Neumann stands out as unique, in the narrow meaning of that abused word, meaning strictly one of a kind. He is, at this time, the only canonized male citizen of the United States.

It is true he was not a native son. His father was born in Bavaria, his mother in Bohemia, and he himself in modern

Czechoslovakia. So he came to America as an immigrant, and became naturalized. But is not this the more to his credit? To be born here is an accident; to come here is a deliberate choice. Bishop Neumann is not an accidental American but a deliberate one.

Besides, he did not come to the United States as many immigrants have. He did not come to better himself, but to offer himself. He left an old and cultured Europe to come to a struggling backwoods — America. There was no thought then of California gold or Texas oil or Pennsylvania coal. Young Neumann did not come with any thought of exploiting America's minerals or exporting its wheat. He came, not to make a fortune but to preach the Good News. He came not to better himself but to offer himself. He came not to get, but to give.

Here is an American who eagerly sought and obtained American citizenship, who worked a quarter of a century under the American flag, who labored in seven American states, who died on an American street, and is buried in an American church in the city of America's Liberty Bell.

He is a man that America needs. If you stroll through the vast museum of America's achievements, you will find many proud exhibits. You will look upon the silver cups of her bronzed athletes, the shining swords and golden epaulets of her famous generals, the bubbling test tubes of her brilliant scientists. But amid this glittering collection, you will look in vain for the relics of an American man who is also a canonized saint.

With dazzling success we have followed all other roads. Till now we have not followed the rugged road whose signpost is the cross. Here, our glorious pioneer is Bishop Neumann. Now our beloved country, hitherto so successful in worldly things, so rich in surgeons and scientists and statesmen and scholars and captains of industry, can now salute a man who is an American and a saint. And, he is one of our own: Saint John Neumann, Redemptorist and American!

The Last Fruit of Tyburn Tree

Most of us know at least a little about Oliver Twist, and perhaps a slight smidgeon about Oliver Wendell Holmes, and maybe too much about Oliver Cromwell. But how many have even heard of Ireland's answer to that last worthy in the person of Oliver Plunket? In a way even the Church lost sight of him, circled though he was with the aura of "blessed." From the gory morn on which he was martyred, back on the first of July 1681, it took nearly three centuries to mature his canonization. In the litany of the saints, put him down as one of the forgotten.

Like many an Irish lad of his era, he felt there was no call higher than the sanctuary. Too, like many another Irish lad, he had an Uncle Pat, but this one happened to be the abbot of a prestigious monastery in Dublin. Abbot Patrick took the boy under his wing, and saw to his youthful education. Then he packed the bright-eyed young man off to the Irish College in Rome, where Oliver majored in theology and minored in lasagna and ravioli.

After eight years of study, the seminarian was ordained. Now, back to his native Ireland and work among his countrymen! So yearned the young priest, but his superiors decided otherwise. His scholastic brilliance would be put to better use, they reasoned, in teaching other seminarians, who in turn would preach the Good News of the Gospel all over the world.

But Oliver Plunket found apostolic outlets beyond the academic classroom. Any free hours he had, took him to the city hospitals — vile places in that primitive day, where gaunt faces stared up from the ward beds and hungered for comfort as well as for cure.

For recreation, the young priest loved to prowl about the tombs of the early martyrs. Did he have a kind of premonition that his own feet were even then marching toward a bloody sunset, and that this communing with the martyrs of yesteryear was really a remote preparation for his own eventual crimson hour?

Just about this time the archbishop of Armagh, the primate of all Ireland, died. It was up to the Pope to find the right replacement. From the various bishops of Ireland the letters poured into the Vatican, suggesting this man or that as the proper man for the post. But Pope Clement IX had already made up his mind. Quite bluntly he said, "Why should I look so far for a candidate, when for the last dozen years I have seen right under my nose the ideal choice? In our very midst is a native Irishman, a man with a brilliant mind, a devout soul, a zealous heart. Here and now I am appointing to the major see of Ireland, Father Oliver Plunket."

This was the way the Pope confided his selection to his advisers, but he dared not make the announcement public. Oliver Plunket got his secret orders but no external celebration. At that time hatred for the Church hovered in many circles like a dark storm cloud, and anti-Catholic spies lurked everywhere. Would you believe that Father Plunket's instructions were to leave Rome, travel incognito to Belgium, and there be raised to the bishopric in an obscure private chapel? Not only that, but the new archbishop was now to proceed on to Ireland under the name of Captain Brown, wearing a powdered wig, sporting a gentleman's sword, and with a brace of gleaming pistols thrust in his belt.

Those were the days in Ireland of the grim Penal Laws. However, the wife of the governor-general (or viceroy) was secretly a Catholic; so out of regard for his wife's feelings, the governor-general allowed the sword of persecution to rust in its scabbard. That was how it was possible for Archbishop Oliver Plunket to stand with miter and crosier and cope in the arch of the great oaken door and take formal possession of his cathedral.

But if he turned around and looked out at the countryside, the bishop would see a landscape of utter spiritual desolation, a countryside where the churches had been destroyed, the schools padlocked, the seminaries emptied and the people (like the early Christians of the Roman catacombs) without bell or building, and with the faith only in their hearts. Some villages had not seen a priest in more than fifty years.

For the new archbishop, the clock did not have enough hours on its dial. From red dawn to black night, Oliver Plunket rode horseback through the rugged hills, baptizing babies, anointing the sick, joining in marriage, administering the sacrament of confirmation (the latter to men and women who were sometimes in their sixties). From his own diary, we know that in his first four years he confirmed forty-eight thousand. The Penal Laws had dried up the stream of the sacraments. He was the first bishop many of them had ever seen.

Alas, the mild viceroy chose this time to die, and his successor lost no time in stirring up the gray embers of persecution. The very first order of the new regime was that all bishops had to leave the country immediately. We know Oliver Plunket's reaction. A letter he wrote to the Pope still survives. It says, "I will not leave. To get me out of Ireland they will have to hang a halter around my neck and drag me to the boat."

For the next six years the archbishop became an outlaw. He was no longer Oliver Plunket. He used any of a half-dozen different aliases. He was no longer, in appearance at least, a clergyman. He was a tinker, an Irish gypsy. He lived in abandoned huts whose thatched roofs were so fallen away he could see the stars or feel the rain. It was a million miles from being anything romantic or dramatic. At times he was in real danger of actually dying from cold or hunger.

The hiding archbishop was never quite sure whom he could trust, and yet he did want to survive, if only for the sake of his flock. For them he said Mass in dark caves or secret meeting places in the hills — always, it seemed, just one step ahead of the king's bloodhounds.

Then he learned that his aged Uncle Pat (the abbot, who

19

for many years now had been the bishop of Meath) was dying. Since Oliver Plunket had been practically brought up by that uncle, he decided to risk a visit so that he could console the old man on his deathbed. It was a brave but fatal mistake.

Some traitor, some lineal descendant of Judas Iscariot, betrayed him. Oliver Plunket had been in Dublin only about a week when a squad of English soldiers battered down the entrance of his hiding place. For six weeks he was locked in solitary confinement in a dungeon, in Dublin Castle. Then came the trial, but the charge (treason against the crown) was so obviously false and the witnesses so obviously lying that even a Protestant jury voted unanimous acquittal.

Still the prosecutor, the earl of Shaftesbury, was determined to get his victim; so he had the case transferred to London. Another trial, and another acquittal! Incredibly they assembled a jury for a third trial. Assembled? Handpicked, rigged is the word. It was enough to make blindfolded Justice drop her scales. This time it took only fifteen minutes to reach a verdict and pass the sentence: death! To which Oliver Plunket responded with head high and voice ringing clear, "Thanks be to God!"

They gave him three days in the Tower of London to get ready, as he phrased it, for "my great day." On execution eve he said, "I have no fear. I believe that Christ by His agony and fear in the Garden of Olives has merited for me to be without fear."

That night he lay down on his prison cot and slept so soundly that he had to be wakened in the morning. Then they took him out and strapped him to a "sledge." This was a low sled dragged by a team of horses. As he bumped and bounced helplessly along the streets, the crowds of spectators hurled insults and garbage at him.

Oliver Plunket was only fifty-two, but hardship made him look more like eighty. The emaciated body, the pale, pinched face, the premature white hair — all showed how suffering had written its diary in deep lines across his holy countenance. But the eyes were serene with inner peace and bright with quiet courage.

At the end of Oxford Street the horses and their jouncing sled came to a halt. Here rose the infamous gallows that was sardonically called "Tyburn Tree." Oliver Plunket was the last human fruit to dangle from it. Perhaps his death, so full of dignity, so majestic in its self-control, gave pause even to those barbarians. Tyburn Tree was civilization at its lowest tide.

They lifted the archbishop to an open cart, and according to custom he spoke his last words. First he solemnly declared his innocence of any treason. Then he forgave them in the words of Saint Stephen, the first Christian martyr: "Lord, lay not this sin to their charge."

After that the hangman looped the bristly rope around the archbishop's neck and dropped the white cap over his eyes. Two soldiers slapped the horses' rumps, the wagon leaped forward, the violent snap broke the victim's neck, and the body swung loosely, feet dancing grotesquely in the air.

Now the crowd, beginning to feel guilty and sick, slunk away. Not even they wanted to see the rest of the barbaric execution sentence: "Drawn and quartered." First a sword was thrust into the twisting body and the heart ripped out. Then the arms and the legs were slashed off, and finally the head hacked off and held up on a pike. This was the way one peeled the fruit of Tyburn Tree. Now do you wonder that Oliver Plunket was the last?

Some who saw him die said that if the saint had lived to preach and work as a bishop for another hundred years he could never have done more for the Catholic faith than he did in that one awful hour of his dying.

It was July 1, 1681. A long time ago, right? Way back in history, wasn't it? But remember, for Oliver Plunket it was not way back in history. For him it was a sunny summer morning, with a sudden, premature sunset, the scarlet sunset of his own martyr's blood. For him it was not way back then, it was the golden now, and he was as much alive as any of us, and he could have stayed alive and gone back to lunch, if only he would have given up the faith. But he was a Christian who followed Christ to the end.

The Not-So-Gentle Jerome

If there is one thing that Saint Jerome liked, it was an argument; so it is ironically appropriate that even the pronunciation of his name is a perennial matter of dispute. Here in the United States we usually call him Je-ROME, with the accent landing like army boots on the second syllable. Our British cousins, however, prefer the stress on "Jer," so that "rome" (like the old bigoted posters) becomes a slurring "rum." Take your choice. Other saints, like Gerard and Bernard, have a similar divided constituency.

At any rate the man behind the name was born around 340 in that section of Italy near the present Yugoslavian border, a region famous for producing fiery spirits. He died far, far away, on the outskirts of Bethlehem where Christ had been cradled three centuries before. Some say Jerome reached seventy-seven, others seventy-eight. In either case it was a fair span between bookends, and one extremely unusual in those uncertain and unmedicated times when so many lives were snuffed out so soon either by bacteria or by brigands.

Born to an affluent family, Jerome received the best education his day could provide. All his life he stayed a bookworm, a mouse of the scrolls, and to the end could spout out long passages of Vergil, Horace, Cicero. In fact Jerome was convinced that one night our Lord appeared to him in a dream with the rebuke, "Jerome, you are not a Christian. You are a Ciceronian!"

Besides Latin, Jerome mastered Greek and Hebrew, the three tools he would need to become the ranking Scripture scholar of his day. But when you mention that he could spray forth a rainbow of languages, you have painted only half the man, and the less interesting at that. The facile linguist was also an even more brilliant controversialist. True, the topics he debated at that time are now only musty pages of forgotten history; but in his turbulent hour they were as contemporary as abortion or drug abuse.

Jerome took on all the current theological giants — including Rufinus and Pelagius — sometimes with a fervor that rose to a fury. He even dared to go after the redoubtable Augustine, not in vocal debate but in an exchange of nineteen letters. Many critics believe that at the bitter end Augustine was licking his wounds while Jerome limped off victorious. There is glory enough for both. If Jerome was the more learned scholar, Augustine was the deeper thinker. Jerome left his mark on the early Church through Scripture, Augustine through philosophy and theology.

Facing a foe in debate, Jerome was about as subtle and as courteous as a column of tanks. The kindest label you can grant him is "outspoken." He pulled no punches and he gave no quarter. He had a wicked wit that could slash like a sword. Armed with the devilish gift of mimicry he was not above imitating an opponent's toothy smile, or his bowlegged walk, or even his hiccups and grunts.

When the debate was on paper, his pen became a bayonet. Of one relapsed heretic he wrote, "Now that the scorpion has died. . . ." Unlike his Savior, Jerome never distinguished between the sin and the sinner. He wanted to grind heresy and heretic alike into the dust. How else explain what he wrote to a priest named Onasus whom he suspected of heretical leanings: "Onasus, the reason you cannot see the truth is that your nose is too big. It shuts out the light from your eyes. So, either cut off your nose or shut your mouth!''

When he stood up to preach, the pulpit became an exploding volcano. He loved to rail against the rich who, he felt, were walking over the defenseless poor. Though never a bishop and only a priest, he delighted in denouncing the soft life of the clergy. He wanted wooden chalices and golden priests, not wooden priests and golden chalices.

In appearance Jerome must have seemed like an Old Testament prophet, an angry man bursting in from the wilderness, black eyes blazing, lips trembling, bringing an urgent message from God. He might begin softly enough, then the gears would shift to purring sarcasm, then the throttle would be wide open and the words would thunder along in a rush of rage. To be fair, though, tolerance and courtesy were not the marks of those primitive times. Manuals of etiquette as well as mouthwashes and deodorants were still far below the horizon.

Not all saints are cast from a bland, plastic mold. They come in all shapes, sizes, colors, temperaments; the only thing common to them is humanity and a deep love of God. Saint Joan of Arc could never be the Little Flower. Between Saint Jerome and, for example, Saint Francis de Sales, stretched a Grand Canyon of difference. Francis de Sales was the polished gentleman — polite, urbane, gracious, moving among the aristocracy as one of themselves. Jerome, on the other hand (who had lived so long in the Syrian wilderness), was rough and tough, irritable and irascible, the hermit of Bethlehem, the hammer of heretics, the lion of the desert. Possessed of a barbed-wire personality he felt more at home among books than among people.

Still, there was in his makeup a certain touch of tenderness, a kind of golden gleam that stole through the somber gray cloud when you least expected it. At the death of Saint Paula, the abbess of a monastery where Jerome had taught the Scriptures, he sat down to write her funeral sermon; the pen fell from his hands and large manly tears blurred the page.

About another younger nun named Sister Fabiola who was gracious and vivacious and invariably pleasant, the tart Jerome for once relaxed into a smile and said, "Fabiola's idea of the stable of Bethlehem would be to make it the annex of the inn. She likes everybody."

The famous portrait of Jerome kneeling in his desert cave and pounding his chest with a stone reveals another side of him. In his diary the saint had written: "Here I am in this bleak wilderness, with its crawling scorpions and prowling beasts. My face is pale from fasting. By day I am scorched by a pitiless sun, and by night I shiver in the cold desert blasts. Yet even then my heart is on fire with the temptation of lust, and my imagination paints before me the dancing girls that I remember when I was young in Rome. So I pray and pray, and beat my breast with a stone, to drive temptation far away. . . ."

From the Syrian desert Jerome moved on to Bethlehem where he founded a monastery which later became the first hostelry in the Holy Land for Christian pilgrims. Now there *would be* room in the inn!

Then, alas, came the Vandals — huge, hairy barbarians with long spears and oxhide shields and flaring torches. Monastery and hostelry crumbled in charred ruins. Mercifully Jerome died just about that time. Eventually his bones were returned to his native Italy and today lie entombed in one of Rome's four famous basilicas, that of St. Mary Major.

It was in Bethlehem that Jerome did much of his major work as a Scripture scholar. The average Catholic, listlessly leafing through his Sunday missalette before Mass, probably never gives a thought to Saint Jerome, but to this man more than to any other he owes his version of the readings. Up there among the Gothic arches and Romanesque curves of stately churches, Jerome's sardonic spirit must smile, because in a sense he wrote the book. His influence pervades the whole Christian world.

Because he lived in the Holy Land itself, Jerome had the supreme advantage of being on the very scene of what he was recording. There he could inquire into the customs, question the inhabitants, and thus give to his writing the impact and the immediacy of a report direct from "our man in Bethlehem."

In his energetic life Jerome achieved three goals: he translated much of the Scriptures; he beat down several rising heresies; and he championed Christian morality in a world that was still swaggering along the garden path of sensual paganism.

Jerome reminded people that it was not enough to know the Bible; you also had to live the Bible. Virtue was not on the page; it was in the soul. In return for his contributions a grateful Church hung on Jerome's warrior chest (albeit posthumously) its two rarest medals. He belongs to that exclusive company called "Doctors of the Church," so called because they have expounded its doctrines so brilliantly. In twenty centuries, less than forty have made that grade. But because Jerome made his contributions to the very early Christian community he is also acclaimed as one of the "Fathers of the Church." This blessed little band is usually reckoned as numbering only eight.

Should you be curious about the other seven (and I hope you are) the Greek wing includes Athanasius, Basil the Great, John Chrysostom and Gregory Nazianzen. The Latin group comprises Augustine, Ambrose and Gregory the Great. (Jerome belongs to the latter group.)

Some saint watchers might evaluate Jerome as a cranky, crotchety, waspish old man who was so passionately devoted to the truth that he frequently lost his temper. But if you measure him against the violent background of his times, the appraisal has to be more compassionate. Had he not seen Rome overrun by the barbarian hordes? Was not this like the bottom dropping out of the civilized world? Furiously the saint gave himself up to saving the only two things worth saving, the Bible and the Church.

Say, if you will, that Jerome was canonized more for his dedication than for his disposition, more for his talents than for his temperament, more for his achievements than for his personality. But the fact still remains that the name of Saint Jerome still soars up, after all these years, as a giant if rugged peak on the mountain range of the first centuries of the faith. We could use his like again.

The Next World's Fair

When New York City hosted its last world's fair the most popular exhibit in that twentieth-century extravaganza was a product of the fifteenth century, Michelangelo's famous statue of our Lady known as the "Pietà." It is sobering to think that he had blown the last little cloud of marble dust from his fingertips when New York was an Indian hunting ground.

But beyond all the technological marvels of our modern age, people flocked to this sculpture from the Renaissance. What does it establish? That the cream will always come to the top? That excellence resists even the gnawing tooth of time? Somehow it makes me think not of the next *world's fair*, but of the *"Next World's* Fair." This will startle many with surprises galore, because it will feature values that this world does not see.

Suppose we take a brief tour of just one corner of this imaginary "Next World's Fair." Here, for example, in this sparkling case is the most unlikely of exhibits. It is an ordinary, ugly, dry, stringy mop. The mother who pushed it is long since dead, but many a midnight she pushed it through the corridors of a New York skyscraper, soaking up the footprints of typists and tycoons. She was helping her boy get through college. The boy is a bishop now, but in God's eyes that long drab mop handle gleams as bright as his golden crosier. It spells love.

Under the very same glass, next to the scraggy, frowsy mop

lies a most unlikely neighbor. It is as beautiful as the mop is ugly: a length of lustrous golden hair, perhaps half a yard long. This is the quiet relic of the day when a young girl marched down the aisle of the convent chapel, all white like a bride, and the bishop's ceremonial shears clicked like a metronome and the burnished locks floated sacrificially to the floor. Then the huge spiked doors groaned open and she entered behind Carmel walls. She wanted to bury herself in Christ, to pray and do penance in secret; but a few years after her death the whole Catholic world knew and loved the radiant childlike nun we call the Little Flower of Jesus, Saint Theresa of Lisieux.

The article in this next cabinet is so small you can hardly see it. It is a railway ticket, in fact only half a ticket, reading in Italian, "Return . . . Rome to Venice." When Cardinal Joseph Sarto stood on the rear platform of the train about to leave Venice for the consistory in Rome to elect a new pope, someone in the crowd shouted out: "Don't forget to come back to us, *Eminenza!*" And the silver-haired cardinal smiled, reached into the depths of his brilliant red robe and waved a ticket. "Have no fear about that," he smiled. "You see I have bought a round-trip ticket."

He never did come back, though. The consistory chose him Pope and he became Pius X. But don't you love the simplicity of a man who never dreamed he would not come back? And don't you love the warm gesture of Pope John XXIII who, when Pius X was canonized and before his body was finally committed to its new marble tomb, sent the remains for a few reverent days to Venice, so that the cardinal after all did keep his word and did come back?

Next in our tiny tour we come upon a rather large glassed-in case with a strange content: a small square wire screen and a few large rocks. The screen is a confessional screen, and against it whispered sins have buzzed like poisonous insects and by its supernatural power fallen dead and harmless. Before its fine mesh, heads that outside tilted tall and haughty, bowed humbly down, and stony eyes blinked back tears. And the rocks? The rocks were the rocks lashed to a sack to weight down the priest's living body that they had crammed into it before dropping the sack into a river and drowning the priest.

You have heard of good King Wenceslaus in the Christmas carol? Well, this murder by drowning involved a bad King Wenceslaus, and when Saint John Nepomucene would not reveal to him the confession of the queen (who, incidentally, was as virtuous as her husband was vile), the king's henchmen gave him one more chance on the bridge of the river Moldau. The saint's head, protruding from the sack, shook silently. He would not break the seal of confession, so they dropped him into the river off the Prague bridge; but the quiet old boast was still true: "Tell the king that I can reach heaven faster by water than he and his gilded coach by land."

We move on through this "Next World's Fair," and here is a strange assortment: the thermometer from a brave little hospital staffed by nuns at the shadowy edge of the African bush; the threadbare white vestment of a priest in a forgotten rural mission in the bleak hills of Wyoming; the long slippery oar pulled by Saint Vincent de Paul when he took a galley prisoner's place. Why are they together? Perhaps because each is a concrete symbol of love for one's fellowman.

But speaking of things that have no apparent connection, under this same section of glass lie a flamboyant purple necktie and a crusty brown whiskey glass. Everybody has heard of Roman collars, but nobody hears of Roman ties, unless by that you mean allegiance to the Pope. But this particular tie — and notice the bullet hole just below the knot — belonged to a Jesuit named Father Miguel Pro. When Plutarco Elías Calles, the dictator of Mexico in the 1920s and 1930s, prohibited priests from practicing the Catholic faith, he should have known that you can easily prohibit but you cannot ever prevent. The priests simply went underground. Father Pro, for example, by day was a crisply dressed, debonair businessman. By night he secretly baptized, absolved, married and preached to little groups like clusters of Christians in the catacombs.

Eventually they caught him and stood him against a wall. He looked into the level line of rifles wearing his smart civilian suit. But when the lieutenant barked, "Ready — aim —" Father Pro shouted, *Viva Cristo Rey!* ("Long live Christ the King!") The shattering volley that followed put a little black period at the end of his words and of his life, but not of his example and his influence. That still streams down, as the poet says, like the light from a long-extinguished star.

And the little brown-stained glass? This was the last glass of whiskey that Matthew Talbot ever touched — Matt Talbot, the Dublin drunkard who bounced from the gutter to the stars and whose cause for beatification is under consideration. Many a time no doubt his hand reached out toward that glass, but resolution like sinews of steel drew it back. It is not a little thing to have been a slave and to become master, master of your own passions, to know the majesty of self-control, and to rule your impulses as an undisputed king in the kingdom of your soul. The secret of all the Matt Talbots and Father Pros in the world is unbudgeable dedication to an ideal.

In the "Next World's Fair" you might expect to find some books, and they are there. One in particular, for instance, was often in the hands of Saint Ignatius of Loyola. Convalescing in a military rest home, a wounded hero for his king, this young captain had finished all the attractive reading available. Then in sheer boredom he turned to the only volume he had not looked into. No wonder. It was a book on the lives of the saints. But because he read with an open heart, something leaped from the pages into his soul. He decided he would henceforth serve the King of Kings. In fact, the book made such an impression on him and so changed his life that he almost made the next edition.

Here is a prayer book with its dainty white cover that looks almost new. No wonder. It saw little use. It was a gift when the girl graduated from grammar school. She found it in a bureau drawer one day thirty years later, and when she thought how in those days she was as pure as a drift of snowy apple blossoms, and how now her soul must look like gray and grimy slush, a tear fell on the open page. It wasn't an idle tear, though. In a way it was like a pearl because it brought her back to confession and helped her save her soul, the pearl of great price.

But what is the moral of this imaginary tour of the "Next World's Fair"? What is the practical lesson for us? Is it not the incisive reminder of Saint Paul that we have not here a lasting city — that while we must make a living we cannot and dare not forget the supreme purpose of life? Where shall we eventually end if we march through this world under the drooping banner of the dollar bill, keeping step to the throb of the world's pagan drums that beat nothing but money and fun, money and fun?

We live in an age that has found the atom and forgotten God. It is an age that is a millionaire in science and a pauper in religion. It is an age of guided missiles and misguided men.

We have to live in the world but we do not have to take our values from the world. Our sights must be set higher, on that next world. It will not have a fair, but it will be there. On God's word.

Brigades in God's Army

As an author, Saint Alphonsus Liguori wrote enough books to fill a small bookcase. As a Doctor of the Church, he was admitted to an ecclesiastical club so exclusive that in twenty centuries it has not tapped forty members. As a moral theologian, he ranked high enough to be declared by Rome the official patron of all confessors.

But golden as these honors are, there are those among us who think he holds an even loftier distinction. To some eight thousand Redemptorist priests and Brothers he is affectionately known as "Our Father," the founder of their worldwide religious community. And, lest wimples crackle in resentment at being coldly overlooked, let it not be forgotten that he also holds a paternal bond with the Redemptoristines, those cloistered nuns whose original vivid habit of red, white and blue gave the patriotic impression that Columbia had taken the veil on the Fourth of July.

Recently the feast day of Alphonsus was nudged back from August 2 to August 1. It makes sense, too, because that was the day on which he died; but at that time, the first of August had long been the feast of Saint Peter in Chains. Just lately this scriptural memorial was suppressed, so Alphonsus regained his death-day for his birthday into heaven.

It is something of a liturgical coincidence that so many founders of religious orders have their feast days during the dog days of August. The founder of the Jesuits, Saint Ignatius of Loyola, just misses the group with his feast day on July 31, but then August goes on to claim founders like Saint Alphonsus, Saint Dominic, Saint John Eudes, Saint Joseph Calasanz, Saint Clare, Saint Augustine and Saint Cajetan.

Another thing. If the historian writes, looking at life through a rearview mirror, Catholic chroniclers have taken advantage of this hindsight to point out how often God has raised up a special religious order to meet a desperate need in an urgent hour. When the barbarians swept across early Christian Europe like a darkening scourge, Saint Benedict's monks of the West not only guarded the light of faith, and sheltered the lamp of learning in the fortresses of their monasteries, but they also eventually sallied forth to civilize and baptize the brawny invaders.

Later, when Christianity took a firmer grip on the little towns and villages and when the church spire rose above the rooftops like an uplifted finger admonishing men about God, when the village church became a more familiar sight — along came the Franciscans in their robes of brown or gray and their slapping sandals to keep the faith fervent. Like spiritual gypsies they plodded the country lanes, sleeping by the side of brooks, hanging their habits on bushes, then pushing on to the next place, always breaking the bread of the word of God to hungry peasants.

Sometimes, in the larger towns and swarming cities this bread of the Gospel grew moldy, tainted by heresy. In France of the Middle Ages the villains were the Catholic Puritans, or as they called themselves, Cathari, meaning pure. They were also known as the Albigenses from the name of the region. Gradually they grew to substantial numbers, and not content with muttering their sour convictions, they preached them from the housetops.

Listen to them and you heard that the body was evil, that marriage came from the devil, and that even the gorgeous panes of the cathedral windows were only sensual traps. But God waved His hand, and into the scene came pouring the white-robed monks of Saint Dominic, the Order of Preachers. These trumpets of truth soon took over the pulpits in the larger towns and the growing cities, and proclaimed the true Christian teaching: that man was essentially good, that life was worthwhile, and that even this sin-scarred world could still be a reasonably happy highway to heaven.

A few centuries later the Protestant Reformation crashed down on the Church like an Alpine avalanche upon a sleeping village. It is hard to estimate the awful impact of this upon Catholicity. Almost overnight a half-dozen nations turned their backs on Rome. The tragedy is that the wreckers tore down the wrong house.

No one denies that there were prelates in those days whose lives, colored with the new paganism of the Renaissance, rose as a hideous stench in the nostrils of heaven. But the reformers, instead of changing the morals of churchmen, attacked the doctrines of the Church. The sacrifice of the Mass and the veneration of Mary, the authority of the Pope and the souls in purgatory, the confessional, the tabernacle, the anointing of the sick — these were some of the casualties when the incense smoke of religious war cleared away.

It is both curious and significant that European Protestantism (which swept into the sixteenth century like a rampaging river) never reached beyond that watermark but from then on only receded. For this a huge segment of the credit must go to the so-called Counter-Reformation. Once again it was a religious order that stepped into the breach, this time the Company of Jesus, under their ex-officer commander, Saint Ignatius of Loyola. These Jesuits soon became known for their intellectual achievement and their military obedience. They founded schools, academies and colleges that stood like breakwaters against the inrushing, roaring tide of the new heresy.

And so you could go on riffling through the pages of history and note the timely appearance of this religious order or that at some critical moment in the Church's life. When the Muhammadans poured into Spain, and in sudden raids carried off whole villages of captives, there rose almost out of nowhere the Order of Trinitarians. Their whole vocation was through prayers and alms to ransom poor Christian slaves from Muslim chains. When Africa was first opened to the white man, a religious order named the White Fathers (because of their tropical white cassock) plunged into darkest Africa to bring the Gospel where it had never been brought before. Some of them became martyrs whose bones lay bleaching on many a jungle trail.

Closer to our time, the Josephites were founded to bring the faith to the black people of the South. The Paulist Fathers had a broader ambition: to invite non-Catholics in the United States into the true fold. Very appropriately their first half-dozen members had been converts from Protestantism. Since then they have done superb work in the convert field. By pulpit and platform and press they have eloquently pleaded with American Protestants to come back to the faith of their forefathers.

This brings us to the Redemptorists, for the Redemptorists were the rock out of which the Paulists were hewn. The original Paulists were all Redemptorists. Many people are under the impression that the Redemptorists are a "German order." This misapprehension came about because a century and a half ago an urgent call came from bishops in America for German-speaking priests to take care of the German immigrants who had poured into places like Cincinnati and Rochester and parts of Pennsylvania. The first Redemptorists to respond hailed from Austria, and no praise is too high for the incredible achievements of these heroic pioneers.

However, the fact remains that a whole century before this, the Redemptorists had been founded in Italy by Saint Alphonsus Liguori. As a secular priest Padre Alfonso had been both saddened and shocked to see so many cassocks whipping through the streets of Naples, while the peasants in the neighboring hills were spiritually neglected and practically abandoned. In the pulpits of the fashionable city-churches, grand preachers braided bright adjectives, spun mythological allegories and, in short, built sermons like wedding cakes of sweet, pious pastry, while the poor starved for the plain bread of the word of God.

So Alphonsus founded the Redemptorists to do what the Redeemer Himself had done, that is, preach the Good News of Redemption to the most abandoned souls. In this spirit the order (or, technically, congregation) has also become a foreign mission society with headquarters in Rome but with branch offices on every continent. From Ireland to India, from Canada to the Congo, more than eight thousand Sons of Saint Alphonsus wear their traditional black habit and tinkling beads, or the tropical version of all white, but always the rosary.

In our day of increased urbanization, the poor and abandoned are to be found not merely in the green hills of Appalachia but also on the gray streets of swarming cities. Here the special work of the Redemptorists is the parish mission. Recently (and unfortunately and illogically as well) the parish mission has become the favorite target of certain snipers who would like to be considered advanced Catholic thinkers. In their curt appraisal, delivered with something between a liturgical frown and a theological sneer, the parish mission is old hat, out of date, over the hill, passé, kaput, finished.

This is idiocy. For what is a mission? It is a series of spiritual exercises emphasizing the eternal truths. It is having the courage to face the stern realities of sin and responsibility. It is daring to look into the perhaps grimy mirror of conscience and then into the grim depths of hell.

If there is a hell, it is both foolish and futile to ignore it, or to pretend that it is air-conditioned. It is also folly to believe in heaven but not believe in hell, because the evidence is no stronger for the one than for the other. That evidence is the solemn word of God. It is inconsistent to say, "Oh, the golden rule is enough religion for me." For where does the golden rule come from? It is an extract from the Sermon on the Mount, and in that Sermon on the Mount our blessed Lord makes five separate references to hell.

As a matter of fact, only a fraction of the modern mission deals with hell. Perhaps what antagonizes many is the mere use of that word: *mission*. To them it stands for an earsplitting, arm-waving, pulpit-pounding tour of some medieval artist's incandescent concept of Satan's red-coaled inferno, and nothing more. But the point is that a post-Vatican II parish mission contains much more, with, incidentally, no such flamboyant tour of hades. For that reason some missionaries prefer to announce their program as a PARISH RETREAT, or a SPIRITUAL RENEWAL, or even a BACK-TO-GOD WEEK. Actually the name is quite unimportant and easily expendable, but pondering the eternal truths is indispensable.

Every pope in modern times has endorsed the *idea* (never mind the *name*) of parish missions. The canon law of the Church (which by the way is still in force) insists that pastors have missions. Our own natural tendency to spiritual backsliding demands missions.

Say, if you like, that missions are hard to make. Say that they entail sacrifice. Say that they are disturbing. Say that they cannot compete with a comfortable evening at home, complete with easy chair, can of beer and color television. Say missions are not attended the way they used to be. But please do not say they are not suited to our times. They are suited to all times because they deal with no special time but with eternity. And they will be out of date and out of style on the morning when sin is.

When Saint Alphonsus, the young Neapolitan nobleman, turned away from the world, he hung his dress sword, in a dramatic Latin gesture, at the Shrine of Our Lady of Sorrows. He left that weapon, we may say, to his Mother. To his sons, the Redemptorists, he left the sharper weapon of the parish mission. This is distinctly *the* Redemptorist work.

on this rock .

Background to Belief

In our English version of the Mass there is a change you may not have noticed. In the Gloria we still say, "We worship you, we praise you for your glory." In the Preface, we still continue, "We do well always and everywhere to give you thanks." But in the Creed a new formula reads, "*We* believe in one God." It used to be "Credo . . . *I believe*."

In a sense this was stronger and better, because it made you realize that while we can praise God together, and thank God together, each man has to believe by himself, in the lonely lighthouse of his own individual soul.

This belief that we Catholics hold, makes us something of a minor mystery to nonbelievers. The average agnostic, standing on the Alpine peak of his airy attitude toward God (he can take Him or leave Him; we hope God in His mercy takes him and does not ever leave him!) — this average agnostic must surely find the average Catholic a confusing puzzle. Across America there are about fifty million Catholics who on the surface are pretty much the same as everyone else. By and large, they are sane and sensible, not flighty or light-headed, but, on the whole, plain-thinking and hardworking normal people.

In brains your Catholic is probably as bright as the next man, in business as practical, in patriotism as loyal, and in politics as divided. (In Boston, Catholics tend to be Democrats; in Philadelphia, Republicans.) But once these Catholics step into the realm of religion they seem to wave good-bye to common sense and college degrees, and are willing to believe in a soul they cannot see, a hell they cannot feel, a grace they cannot grasp and in a Trinity they do not even try to understand. They appear to check their intelligence at the vestibule of the church, and march in to behave in a benighted, medieval way as if this were not the age of penicillin and computers and space trips.

To a Catholic, however, the picture hangs in a different light, the picture called "faith." To him the frame of the picture is humility. He acknowledges at the start that he is not omniscient. In the Middle Ages a certain smug scholar wrote a book modestly titled *De Omni Re Scibili* (or *All About Everything That Can Be Known*). The man of faith is the first to admit that he does not know everything, but he believes in a God who does. He also is convinced that if God could create him, He could also communicate with him, and we call that communication "revelation."

Knowledge comes to us from one of two sources. We know something for certain (or we accept it as true) either because we were there ourselves (we were in the ball park when Reggie Jackson hit that last home run, or we were in the boat when little Bobby caught the twenty-pound bass) or, if we were not there, we get our information directly or indirectly from somebody who was.

Did Napoleon ever live? Did George Washington ever die? When and where were we ourselves born? The vast majority of our information, perhaps at the ratio of ten thousand to one, comes to us from faith in someone else. In the matter of the Catholic faith, that someone is God, and His human instruments (in this case the writers of the Gospels, the Epistles and the Acts of the Apostles).

So the men to call to the stand are the authors of these documents. They were there on the scene. Mark and Luke, while not Apostles, wrote respectively for Peter and for Paul. But the main point is that the authors of the Gospels were writing about public events, not something hidden but something that took place under the spotlight of the sun — events that took place before hundreds of eyes, events that never were denied by the enemies of Jesus (though they tried to do away with Lazarus as an embarrassing piece of evidence of Christ's power), events that no subsequent research has proved false. In fact, the deeper the spade of the archaeologist plunges into the past the more background facts he turns up to substantiate the Gospel truth.

But what about the character of these witnesses? If they were not deceived, were they possibly themselves deceivers? But no one has ever been able to impute to them the least dishonesty. What motive could they possibly have had to falsify the facts or to distort the truth? Money, like royalties on the Gospels? The Gospels were not collected till after their deaths, and of course there was no printing anyway. Popularity, prestige, prominence? But all they got, and they knew they were asking for it, was persecution. They were opposing the two great powers of the day, the Jewish religion and the Roman Empire — and to oppose the first meant ostracism, and the second, treason.

Has their accuracy been challenged? The four Gospels were written at different times and in different places, and you find precisely what you might expect in such a situation: absolute agreement about the essential major events and minor discrepancies about unimportant details. The writers were not composing scientific treatises, nor orderly historical narratives; they were announcing the Good News of Salvation and they appealed to the miracles of the Savior.

They knew that only the searching glance of God could make water blush into wine. They knew that only the commanding voice of God could make a foaming, raging sea lie down serene as a pool in a park. They knew that only the unique feet of God could walk across the Lake of Genesareth as casually as if it were a blue plush rug. They knew that only the unspeakable power of God could stir His own lifeless body, buried these three days in the tomb, into radiant and victorious life.

Shall we reject all this testimony (and a score of other dazzling miracles) merely because we cannot comprehend how it was done? *I* cannot understand it; therefore, God could not have done it. This is logic?

Consider, furthermore, the incredible aftermath of these wonders. If the Gospels were only a naive fairy tale or a monstrous fraud, how far do you think Christianity would have got?

A young officer once flippantly said to Napoleon, "I am getting tired of this Catholic religion. It is too strict. I think I'll start a new religion." "Fine!" answered Napoleon. "For a start, get yourself killed. Stay in the grave three days. Then rise."

Apart from that impossibility, it is quite conceivable that a man could launch a new religion. Let him have enough money to finance it, enough influence to establish it, and, above all, let it be a religion which appeals to all the weaknesses of poor old human nature. Let its commandments be soft as marshmallows, its laws mere silken threads which passion could snap with a chuckle. Such a religion a sensual and indulgent world might receive eagerly, and it might prosper widely.

But does this describe the birth of Christianity? If Christianity had a letterhead, the names of the board of directors would be a rude, crude, ignorant, illiterate band of peasants, still reeking of fish scales. They had no education, they had no wealth, they had not an eyedropperful of influence. Once they left their native place to preach abroad, they were scowled at as enemy aliens. Further, they preached a Gospel whose roots were Jewish in a world that was proudly Roman or stylishly Greek. They preached a Gospel of purity in a world that was so pagan that vice was a virtue and virtue a vice. They preached a Gospel that advocated forgiveness of enemies in a world that sought only sweet, satisfying revenge.

Yet this religion, despite ten separate persecutions, each one

41

aimed at annihilating it, and after three centuries of bloody am-
phitheaters and armies of martyrs, somehow spread across the
civilized world. Was there not behind it a power more than
human?

Still, all the arguments in the world can never make a man
believe. The evidence goes only so far; good will has to take the
remaining step. Ultimately, faith is a gift of God. It comes to
those who ask. It stays with those who cherish and practice it.

The Indispensable Man

Each year on the twenty-second of February, the United
States remembers (though often without a holiday) the birthday
of its first president. Each year on the same date, the Catholic
Church remembers with only a minor feast day its first pope.

The feast is called "The Cathedral of Saint Peter." This
does not refer to the physical structure of that famous church. It
celebrates rather Saint Peter's establishing himself in Rome as
bishop. "Cathedral" literally means a chair, not a church, and
here stands for the chair of authority.

That notion of authority is important. The average Catholic
does not love the hard things in his religion. Being a normal
human being, and tainted with original sin, he is not by nature
enthusiastic about such things as Lenten penance, the obligation
of Mass every Sunday, the need of humble confession, the doctrine of an everlasting hell.

He sees people of other faiths following an apparently
plushier path toward the same Pearly Gates, and he wonders if
he too should not kick off his hobnailed hiking boots and slip
into more comfortable moccasins. Why not switch from hot to
cool, from the hard and the harsh to the less demanding and the
more relaxing?

So, if a Catholic does not want to be a first-grade fool, if he does not want to thrust his head into the stocks reserved for the village idiot, he ought to be a good deal surer than Westinghouse that his Church is the true Church, and has the authority to make such demands. He should know why it has the right to lay down such unpleasant and unpopular prohibitions as no divorce and no abortion and no artificial contraception.

Where does the Church get its authority? Certainly not merely from its age, though it is centuries old. Certainly not from its size, though it stretches around the globe. Certainly not from its ritual, though at its best this is glittering pageantry. It is well enough for the pulpit orator to grow rhetorical and proclaim in lyrical outbursts that the Catholic Church is the scarlet robe of the stately cardinal and the rumpled black cassock of the drowsy altar boy, the majestic spires of the European cathedral and the thatched chapel of the African missionary, the devout scientist like Pasteur leaving his test tubes to pray in Notre Dame, and the baby wailing for its bottle at the baptismal font. But these are only picturesque details. They are only colorful petals of the flower. For the authority of the Church you have to go deep down to the strong, hidden roots of human reason and biblical history.

Which brings us back to February 22 and the feast of Saint Peter. Originally Peter was a fisherman named Simon. Then one historic day the Savior gave him a new name. The word that Jesus used was probably the Aramaic *Kefa*, which became the Greek *Cephas*, and the Latin *Petra* — but they all mean *Rock*. Incidentally, it should be stressed that this was the same Christ who had praised a wise man for building his house not on shifting sands but on solid rock, so that when the storms came and the winds blew and the rains lashed, the house did not collapse or sway or even budge.

The words of Christ are simplicity itself: "You are Peter [the Rock] and on this rock I will build my Church. And the gates of the underworld [the forces of evil] can never hold out against it" (Matthew 16:18). So Peter was to be the foundation of the Church. But the Church was not to be a single material building. It was to be a group of followers, and in this sense Peter was not to be the bottom (like the foundation of a building), but the top, the ruler, the head.

This is not just a logical conclusion. Christ went on to make this very point radiantly clear. He added, "I will give you the keys of the kingdom of heaven: whatever you bind on earth shall be considered bound in heaven; whatever you loose on earth shall be considered loosed in heaven" (Matthew 16:19). In the time of Jesus a ring of keys was the symbol of authority. Jesus was thus giving Peter complete authority over His Church, saying that whatever laws in the realm of religion that Peter made on earth, these would be ratified in heaven.

However, Christ knew that He would have to leave the earth, and He knew that Peter too would die. Yet the Church was to go on for all generations still to be. So He had solemnly assured the Apostles that He would be with them always, until the end of the world. By this sacred promise, our divine Savior pledged that He would be with Peter and his successors to the end of time, protecting them against any serious error in faith or morality.

Both reason and experience demonstrate that for a church to teach the truth unswervingly through the ages it must have an infallible guide. Without such certitude, doctrine becomes surmise rather than certainty; it becomes anybody's guess rather than God's will. Soon you have nothing but a kind of holy hash, or a spiritual stew of many pious brainstorms, and all sorts of religious experiments.

Take the matter of bishops. In the beginning, Peter was bishop of Rome, and the other bishops were subject to him. But gradually the city of Rome lost its imperial prestige. In wealth, in culture, in power, it fell into pathetic decline. Meanwhile, in the East, Constantinople became a rich and magnificent metropolis.

Soon it began to wonder why the head of the Church should be in shabby Rome, while Constantinople had only a patriarch. Let there be, it urged, not just one pope in Rome, but two equal patriarchs — one in Rome and one in Constantinople.

Later on, at the beginning of the Reformation, the cry went up (and Henry the Eighth cheered this proposal): "Let there be neither pope nor patriarchs, but only bishops!" Then, as the Reformation got going in Germany, the tune grew louder. Now it was no pope, no patriarch, no bishops, but only pastors. Finally, by the time it had reached America, the slogan had become: "Let there not even be pastors, but only preachers!"

Thus crumbled the original concept of a Christian Church, and small wonder when you remember that in the United States alone there were some two hundred different denominations claiming to be the true Church of Christ. Can anyone believe that this fragmented, jigsaw puzzle of faiths was what Christ had meant when He said, "On this rock I will build my Church"? Not Churches; *Church*. Without His protection and guidance, even the rock would have become gravel.

Some may protest that nowhere in the Scripture will you find the word "pope." For that matter, nowhere will you find the word "Protestant" or even the word "pulpit." The word, the term, does not matter. What you do find is the fact, the thing, the office, the man, the authority, the rock, the keys, the promise of Christ.

Or others may demur that the Church is so different today from the days of the Apostles. But this difference is in the incidentals, not in the essentials. Sometimes in a magazine you will see a picture of a child in rompers and the question, "What famous actor or politician is this?" Usually, you are completely at a loss, because the man of thirty-two or fifty-two looks entirely different from the child of two. But the fact is that they are still the same person.

Wherever you have life, you have some sort of change.

What a far cry from Washington's headquarters at Valley Forge to the modern Pentagon! Yet they are both fundamentally the same thing, our military headquarters. A rifleman of the Revolution in his buff and blue and with his musket and powder horn would stare in amazement at a Marine pilot in pressure suit and oxygen mask. Yet they both are the same American military, fighting under the same flag (with a few more stars) and defending the same country.

In the same way, a bishop of the third century would certainly look blank if you showed him a cardinal's red hat or a nun's brown scapular. But these too are only external fringes of the Church, mere fripperies that could be clipped off without doing any harm to the main fabric. They are not doctrines, only decorations. The Church could go on without missing them, as indeed for many centuries it did, and in some future century it well may.

But what the bishop of the third century would recognize, with a warm and welcoming eye, would be the essentials of the Church, like the baptizing of babies and the forgiving of sins and the anointing of the sick and the bread and wine of the Mass.

And he would certainly recognize, as bishops of his era (like Irenaeus, Eusebius, Epiphanius) did, that the bishop of Rome was the successor of Saint Peter and the head of the Church. After all, it is the name Peter that heads every list of the Apostles. It was Peter for whom Christ prayed as a special person. It was Peter to whom Christ appeared individually after the Resurrection. It was Peter who first preached the Gospel on the birthday of the Church at Pentecost. It was Peter who presided at the Council of Jerusalem. And, above all, it was Peter to whom the Savior said, "Feed my lambs, feed my sheep."

And it is the successors of Saint Peter at Rome who have been at the helm of Peter's ship ever since. To weather the storms of this world, God knows we need an infallible guide! God knows? God knew, and that is why He gave us a pope.

The Flickering Lantern of Luther

The late Redemptorist bishop, William T. McCarthy (T for Tiburtius, he would occasionally admit), used to have a way of expressing simultaneous surprise and disapproval by tilting back his huge head and pursing his lips in a pained, noiseless whistle. The last time I saw this "Non Imprimatur" in action was shortly before his death. There had been a play about Martin Luther, and a movie, and a couple of articles in which Catholic writers had swung laudatory thuribles. The bishop gave his breathy whistle and grunted, "Now they want to canonize Luther!"

I thought of that the other day when I saw the parishioners open their missalettes to Luther's "A Mighty Fortress Is Our God," and smiled again when later that week I came upon the same hymn in my own breviary. Ecumenism, like the ladies, has come a long way. It nudges the tiny wonder whether there are any similar Catholic stanzas on the pages of Protestant hymnals.

It made me start reading again about Luther, and the more I read about this complex character, the more I was mystified and perplexed. For every plus, there appears to be a balancing minus. You just about start to sympathize with him when you come upon something that makes you frown. And the bottom line is only a pointless sigh: If only he had used his incredible energy, his volcanic oratory, his flaming zeal for reform, inside the Church, instead of leaving it via excommunication!

He was a black-cowled Augustinian monk the day he raised his wide, flowing sleeve and tacked those defiant theses on the church door at Wittenberg. Incidentally, he could hardly have been reprimanded for defacing the panels, because this was the university's bulletin board, already scarred with many a nail print. Luther was merely making use of the conventional summons to ecclesiastical debate. There was, though, a touch of clerical showmanship in flinging up his little billboard on Halloween, because the next day everybody would be pouring through those doors on the way to Mass (including his Mass) for the great feast of All Saints.

His ninety-five theses (and nobody then suspected they were the first distant boom of a long war against the Church) blazed out a broadside against indulgences. No historian worthy of his footnotes has ever doubted that in this particular area there had been many howling abuses. Popular preachers with spread-eagle oratory had tried to "push" certain indulgences with outbursts and overtones that managed to be both superstitious and mercenary, and the Church had done too little to stop them. The remote purpose of the appeal was good — namely, the rebuilding of St. Peter's; but the road definitely took some weirdly crooked turns.

Almsgiving is a legitimate form of atonement, but nobody can ever just buy heaven. The Church never has taught and never can teach such comforting nonsense as that an indulgence (just by itself) can wipe away the guilt of past sins, or the even more alluring come-on that such an indulgence will also take care of any sins one might commit in the future. This was putting the carte blanche before the horse sense. It was heresy on the half shell, visible and tangible, and not to be swallowed without a bad case of theological ptomaine.

Had Luther been content only to loose his angry artillery against such outrageous errors and such venal exploitation, he would have been right on target. He would have been standing on solid Catholic ground and would have rated ringing historical applause. Unfortunately, he moved on.

From attacking abuses, Luther proceeded to attack doctrines. Like a new Samson, tugging at the pillars of the temple, he began to pull down some tall basic truths, including the reservation of the Blessed Sacrament, the priesthood, the office of bishops, the papacy. In their place would rise a new central teaching: justification by faith alone.

Who was right? The Catholic Church had been teaching its

truths for almost fifteen hundred years. If the Church were wrong, had not Christ let it wander through the woods of error all these long centuries? But He had promised to be with the Church all days. Had He gone back on His word? Was the first gleam of true Christianity now glinting in the pen of a former monk named Martin Luther? And this more than a thousand years after Christ had gone?

There is little reason to doubt *why* Luther raised the standard of revolt. He never wrote an early autobiography, "I Was A Teenage Catholic," but if he had, he could have stressed that in his early, adolescent years the Pope on the throne of Peter was Alexander VI, who roughly stood in relation to the papacy as Judas did to the Apostles, or Benedict Arnold to the Continental army. No one ever challenged Alexander's ability or even his orthodoxy, but his shadowed life is scarcely required reading in a nuns' novitiate.

Tracking muddy boots across the marble sanctuary (at least in his pre-papal days), Alexander VI died when Luther was a young, impressionable twenty. The next man to sink comfortably into the Chair of Peter was the worldly Leo X, whose inaugural address is alleged to have been: "Now that God has given us the papacy, let us enjoy it!"

Surely it was a time to try the patience (if not the faith) of any eager idealist, especially, if like Luther, the business of your order took you to Rome, and there you saw with your own scandalized eyes the festering internal corruption. This was the scarlet-and-gold age of the Renaissance, when everything flourished except the faith, when pagan art and pagan literature were being showcased, and when a grim moral darkness dropped down around Christian Rome like the Good Friday darkness around Calvary.

Luther saw empurpled prelates living as if they were secular princes whose profession emphasized religious pageantry. It was truly an evil hour. But if Jesus Christ in His own company had a doubting Thomas, and a denying Peter, and a betraying Judas, could the Church expect to fare better than its Founder? Essentially it was still holy, but all that Luther saw were the spiders crawling around the holy-water font.

Surely there was need for a reformation, but a reformation of morals, not of doctrine, a reformation of churchmen, not of the Church. Luther should have leaped into the saddle and leveled his lance against a simony that bought bishops' miters with depraved money, against a nepotism that took care of incompetent nephews, against a general laxity that reduced the Vatican to the level of just another royal court.

But instead of going after the wild ones among the few, Luther decided to remodel the ship and revise the course. It is undeniable that popes like Alexander VI and Leo X were sorry specimens of papal timber, but on the other hand the papacy itself, coming directly from Christ Himself, was still like a precious jewel which does not lose one whit of its essential value even if for the moment it lies in a pitiful human setting of rusty tin.

Apparently Luther could not see the distinction. He was not so much a man for subtleties as of contradictions. Now he faces in one direction, and then comes a whistling wind, and he veers to the opposite quarter. As a young monk, he was tortured by scruples about purity. Later on, he swung around to holding the practical impossibility of being continent. Concupiscence was irrepressible. In line with this, he urged Henry VIII to deal himself another queen in the attractive form of Anne Boleyn, even though the king had been duly wed to Katharine of Aragón. Treading the same earthy path, Luther allowed the Landgrave of Hesse to take a second wife along with his first. Luther cut his own vow of chastity like a thin ribbon and became the husband of a former nun named Katharina von Bora. Even so, Women's Lib could hardly hail as a hero the man who bluntly said, "Women are made to be either wives or prostitutes."

In the matter of language, it has been claimed that no one,

with the exception of Goethe, has had more impact on the German tongue than Luther. Grant that, and then reflect that Luther's own conversation, as reflected in his *Tischreden* (or *Table Talk*) is so coarse and foul-mouthed that no family newspaper would reprint it today.

Or consider another contradiction. Largely because of Luther's flaming rhetoric, the peasants rose against their masters. Luther had not anticipated such a wild uprising, so he pleaded with them to go back and follow their old furrows, and lay down their angry scythes and crackling torches. But it was too late. So Luther, in another about-face, urged the nobles to beat down the rebellion, "to hang, burn, behead, and torture, to keep the people in check." Yet, when he was dying, he lamented that his followers had become "seven times more scandalous than any of their predecessors."

"Search the Scriptures!" was Luther's sacred slogan. What helped to send this Bible emphasis flying across the land on paper wings was the recent invention of printing. But how often are you told that Luther was by no means the first to put the New Testament into German? Would you believe that there had been nineteen prior Catholic editions? Luther's distinction was that he blanketed the field.

When he said, "Search the Scriptures!" he meant that the truth was there for any man to read, and there was no need for Pope or Church to interpret what any particular text might mean. Private interpretation was the name of the game. And yet (still speaking of contradictions) when men like Carlstadt and Calvin and Zwingli dared to differ with him, Luther suddenly became his own pope, Martin the First, and proclaimed what was the indisputable, infallible truth. For some curious reason, his foes would not accept it, and almost from the beginning the Lutheran Church split wide open.

In this respect, it is quite possible that many a crisp and brisk modern has never thought of the origins of our New Testament. Does he really believe that one fine morning it was delivered in the early mail, elegantly bound and handsomely boxed? The truth is, of course, that during the first years of Christianity, there were dozens of spiritual documents bouncing around the young Christian communities. What we now accept as the New Testament is the selection from these parchments made by the early Church.

What was it that kept Martin Luther from being another Saint John Chrysostom? He had the same brilliant mind, the same vivid oratory, the same complete dedication, the same cool personal courage, the same raging zeal for what he thought was right.

There are several answers, but the simplest is that Martin Luther, instead of just blasting the contemporary unworthy popes, wanted to destroy the office itself. His favorite name for the papacy was "The Donkey." More than anything else, he would like to see the Donkey bray no more.

But did he forget that Christ came riding into Jerusalem on a donkey, and could (if He so willed) go riding through history on a donkey? The person of any pope is not important. Peter the First, liar and denier, died. So did Alexander VI, and Leo X; but the long white line moves quietly on. Perhaps someday one of these will crawl out of a bomb shelter and begin with the catacombs all over again. The promise still holds: "Know that I am with you always; yes, to the end of time" (Matthew 28:20). That Light will always burn.

Too Much Religion?

The young couple came to the rectory to arrange their marriage, but somehow gave the impression that they would not be too disappointed if the marriage took place not before a church altar but before a City Hall desk. Yes, this was her parish, but she did not come here regularly to Mass. In fact, she did not go regularly anywhere. Sunday, she explained with a silly simper, was like checkers. She jumped quite a few spaces. It was gently suggested that she might really be playing another game, hide-and-seek with God, and that eventually He might grow tired of looking and forget to find her. This drew a derisive toss of her shoulders and the remark, "I suppose I got too much religion as a child in the old country."

It turned out that her parents had insisted she go to Mass every Sunday and every holy day of obligation. So, going to church in Ireland took the rap for not going to church in America. Somehow, it reminded one of the drinker who woke up with a horrible hangover after nine martinis and blamed the olives. It is so easy to be blind and pin the blame anywhere but on the donkey that ought to wear it.

Too much religion? Not *genuine* religion. Genuine religion makes a person more devoted to God, not less. And genuine religion is always reasonable. It is not genuine religion, for example, for the mother of a family to traipse off to Mass each morning if this means that the husband and children will have to rustle up breakfast while she rattles her beads. It is not genuine religion to spend any time at all in church that should be devoted to keeping the home neat and clean. It is not genuine religion to drag a little child to church and hold him there, restless and squirming and utterly unhappy, while the mother mumbles her endless prayers. It is not genuine religion to take a twelve-year-old and try to drape over him a pattern of piety that would better become a sedate nun.

But, honestly, how often do these excesses or abuses occur? Not half so often as they are trumped up as excuses for abandoning religion! Listen to some people who boast that now they do not darken the door of a church, and you get the impression that as children they were scourged to Mass at the end of a long crackling whip. But ask a little further, and you discover that this big bubble-gum blob of complaint that overflows their mouths collapses into the simple quiet admission that their mother and father insisted that the children attend their ordinary religious duties. The children were not martyrs, and the parents were not tyrants.

Is it tyranny to demand that the children go to Mass on Sunday, attend their religious class or Confraternity of Christian Doctrine during the week, and go to confession once a month, say for the First Friday? Does supervising the ordinary routine of a normal good Catholic family constitute cruelty to children, because the children, if left on their own, would prefer to skip it all? Is this what is called forcing religion down a child's throat? Then why force the child in other fields? Since he would also rather miss school, why keep him cooped up in a cramped classroom instead of letting him merrily roam the streets?

It all comes down to this: Who is to decide what is for the child's good? The parents who have the responsibility for his religious training, or the youngster himself who would cheerfully vote against both catechism and vegetables, who is not too keen about saying his prayers or washing behind his ears, who is about as enthusiastic about confession as he is about vaccination? There are so many things that the child would rather not. But the parents know that certain things are good for him, like training in religion or learning to read or studying geography. In most homes, too, the danger of too much religion is about as grave as the danger of too much geography. Of all the alibis adduced for shortchanging the Lord in later life, the most childish is that as a child someone was so stuffed with God, as with green apples, that he has been sour on Him ever since.

Speaking of sour, the boyfriend with the saucy colleen now began to snap his slingshot and pop his little pebble at the Church. He believed that religion put people under too great a strain. Presumably he meant other people, for aside from the impression that he was ill at ease in these rectory surroundings, he seemed under no strain himself. He was rather bluff and breezy, with a manner that was as loud as the flamboyant blazer he wore. He seemed the very image of the twentieth-century pagan who has just lifted the lid from life, found it duck soup, and was about to attack it with no holds barred. No religion for him, thank you. Religion was altogether too depressing, too confining, too restrictive. It flung up a fence around man's freedom; it tied a heavy weight to a man's natural desires; it threw a dark shadow over what ought to be golden days.

This was not precisely his phrasing, but these were exactly his ideas. He wanted to be perfectly free, with none of the awkward prohibitions like the commandments of God or the laws of the Church. But, you could not help thinking, what a weird world it would be, if all its departments were run the way he wanted them run in the realm of religion or morality! Down would come, of course, the traffic lights, because they were admittedly restrictive and frustrating and irritating. Out would go all the ledgers and account books of business offices, because it was surely a strain to keep strict account of profits and losses, debits and credits. And, while you are at it, take up the buoys and the lights from the channel, because especially in a storm it is certainly something of a strain to make sure you steer between them and do not run aground.

But is it not all too foolish to consider? Granted that the modern pagan who ignores morality is under no strain, the liberty he enjoys is only the liberty of the libertine, meaning he is like a kite that has snapped its string and is plunging wildly about all over the sky, but which eventually, precisely because it has no restriction, no mooring, is bound to drop to pitiful ruin.

Anyone who is doing anything worthwhile is always under some sort of strain. Not the tramp, who drifts aimlessly from town to town, like a dead leaf before the wind; he is under no strain. But the father of a family is, because he is tethered to his job and his home. The surgeon is under a strain from the moment he touches the scalpel. The anesthetist sits on the very edge of anxiety studying his dials. The jet pilot does not break out in a booming baritone as he lands his airplane. Wherever there is serious responsibility, there is bound to be some strain.

This holds for religion too. God has given us commandments and obligations that do not exactly promote giggles or produce playboys. The question is not what is the most nonchalant attitude we can adopt toward life, or what code of conduct will give us the least concern, but what course has God, through His Church, laid out for us?

And the answer, whether we like it or not, is that God has not given us a religion based on low standards, broad views and high spirits. How can a man's moral and spiritual life be a bed of roses when the Gospels bristle with such thorny texts as, "Lay the ax to the root!" and "Take up your cross and follow me!"

Naturally we all prefer easy things. It would be pleasant if hell were air-conditioned, and if each spike of the picket fence of the commandments were sheathed with soft plush, and if allowances were made for at least cultured and refined sin, a kind of discreet immorality in moderation.

Notice, however, that the Savior who was willing to forgive any really repentant sinner never had even one kind syllable to say about sin itself. How seldom we recall the angry Christ whose arm swung the knotted scourge in the temple, and whose voice roared, "Thieves!" It is doubtful if the money changers whom He drove out that day, for defiling His Father's house, gathered at the bottom of the temple steps and serenaded Christ with, "For He's a jolly good fellow!"

We have drifted a long way from the two people in the rectory parlor, haven't we? No matter. It turned out that the young man had been married before, for six months, and was divorced. The pair would have preferred to be married in the Church for the sake of his mother, who was a devout Catholic. They were fairly sure they could not, and hence their hostile stance. So this was what was wrong — not that she had had too much religion in Ireland, and not that he felt religion put people under too great a strain, but simply their own present personal situation. What was wrong was not with the Church, but with themselves. Isn't this generally the way?

through the year

Christmas Afterthought

In one seminary on Christmas Eve morning we were clanged out of bed at five o'clock the same as on any other day. However, the rest of the day was devoted not to classroom lectures but to decorating the chapel and the refectory and the huge community room. We hung wreaths and tacked up streamers till spots of red and green danced before our eyes. At 8:30 in the evening we were sent to bed (grown men) to rest for a few hours before Midnight Mass.

At 11:30 that night the quartet of great bells in the tower began to turn handsprings, bonging and banging enough to shake the frosty stars. At 11:45 the seminary choir marched slowly through the corridors, roaring out carols right outside our rooms with a vigor that roused perhaps louder echoes than did the angels over Judean hills.

At five minutes before midnight the electric gong on each floor sent its metallic whir through every corner of the building, all but vibrating the pictures off the walls. By this time everybody was hurrying along toward the chapel which was, thanks to our labors, a spectacular blaze of gorgeous decorations.

Well, not quite everybody. I had managed to sleep through everything. The first sound I heard was the late rising bell (at six!) on Christmas morning. Even then, as I joined the others hurrying along toward the chapel there was never a doubt in my mind but that we were on our way to Midnight Mass. Then I noticed that I was the only one carrying a gradual, the big book we used at High Masses. I looked up at a clock (watches were a forbidden luxury till we were ordained) and saw the horrible truth. The clock said twenty past six.

Even then I had a problem. I wanted to receive Communion, but not conspicuously alone in front of the entire student body. Singularity was something the authorities were always frowning on and thundering against. So I drifted over to a side altar where one of the young student-priests was vesting, offered to serve his Mass and shyly asked if I might go to Communion too. He smiled patiently and explained, as with a none-too-bright child, that I had already received Communion at the Midnight Mass, and although that might have seemed like last night it had actually happened early this morning, and no one could receive twice on the same day. When I explained that I had slept through the tower bells, the electric bell, even the silver-bell voices of the choir, he just stared in dumb disbelief. I can still see Father Breslin's head soundlessly shaking back and forth like an incredulous windshield wiper.

So I missed Midnight Mass, but not Mass, and above all, not Christmas. Or don't you believe that many Christians still miss Christmas? Is it too harsh to say that some celebrate only a holiday called the twenty-fifth of December? And with all their celebration they are not really and deeply happy? It is one of life's beribboned little ironies that it is perfectly possible to spend a miserable Christmas in the plushiest Park Avenue penthouse, surrounded by glittering islands of expensive gifts. On the other hand it is possible to spend a thrilling Christmas even in a stable. I believe once it was actually done.

For what really makes Christmas? Some years ago a big New York store displayed a series of fascinating Christmas windows. The first window carried a long scroll that read: "The smell of Christmas is in the kitchen," and you saw an old-fashioned black stove with simmering pots and sizzling pans and fragrances curling up from each. The second window said, "The taste of Christmas is in the dining room," and you saw the white cloth and the gleaming silver and the lighted candles and the festive table that looked like a feast for a king. The next window said, "The color of Christmas is in the tree," and you saw a tall green tree, proud as a bride, wearing its ornaments like loops and loops of jeweled necklaces. The fourth window announced, "The sound of Christmas is in the carols," and there was a group of puppet children, gay mufflers flung back and pink cheeks puffed out, singing the tinkling songs of the season.

Then came the big store's main entrance with swishing doors and swarming people. If you entered the store then and there, you had seen your last Christmas window. But if you ignored the entrance to the merchandise mart and kept going, you saw on the other side a narrow oblong window that said, "But the heart and soul of Christmas is here," and there was a radiant painting of Mary, the Madonna of Bethlehem, with the Christ Child cradled in her arms.

In a way those windows were a Christmas homily in themselves. It reminded you that our modern Christmas can be so merry in its celebration and so wrapped up in the bright packages of its commercialization that you have to look consciously for the real meaning, the essence, the core of Christmas. Is this season dedicated to attractive gifts scattered under a green tree, or to a tiny Child lying on yellow straw? Is it all about handsome presents wrapped in crinkly holiday paper, or about a Baby wrapped in swaddling clothes?

Last Christmas I saw a little girl who had just reached the magic age of four and who was fingering the dark green boughs of a Christmas tree that had just been delivered to her home. Her grandfather was saying to her, "Judy, this tree has come all the way from a big forest hundreds of miles from here, a place called Maine, just to bring Christmas to you!" Judy looked at the tree again, and this time her eyes were like two of the big shining

60

balls that would soon be hanging from it. She was more than impressed. She was awed.

Maybe our old eyes would shine too if we could bring ourselves to remember that Christmas comes to us all the way from a sacred spot called Bethlehem, and from a holy night hundreds and hundreds of years ago. On that first Christmas, nobody was concerned with holly wreaths or jolly Santas or greeting cards or gift catalogs. All attention funneled down like the light of the star on a bleak cave and a helpless Child.

This is the heart of Christmas. That Child is still with us. For the faithful, Christmas is not just an anniversary, but is something contemporary. We still have Christ in our midst, Immanuel (God with us), on our altar!

Admittedly, nobody dreamed of the Mass or of the Blessed Sacrament that first Christmas night. Peter was just a stripling lad, maybe taking his first moonlit trip on the Sea of Galilee. Perhaps as the waves rolled gently by, each glassy hollow was filled with golden moonbeams till it looked like a manger filled with glinting straw; but surely Peter never thought of that. And yet, across that sea and far away from Peter's town of Bethsaida, in an even smaller village named Bethlehem, there lay at that moment in the manger the Messiah who would one day make Peter the head of His Church. The Child who was even now lying in the feed-trough of the cattle would on another sacred night sit down at the table of the Last Supper, take bread and whisper: "This is my body," and command Peter and his companions, "Do this in memory of me!" The first holy night He would be born deep down in a cave; but on that last holy night of His life, high in the upper room, He would arrange never to die, at least in the sense that He would never leave us.

Christmas just serves to remind us that He is here. Look at the Christmas crib in the church. Certainly it is charming, it is picturesque, it is devotional, it is even touching. But at best it is only a kind of pious nostalgia for a Bethlehem that was; it is devout make-believe, it is pageantry, it is playacting. The figures are plaster, the straw is artificial and fireproof, the manger is a miniature souvenir. If you want reality, if you want the true living Christ, look to the altar!

If you seek the rocky cave, there it is in the marble tabernacle. If you seek the flaming Christmas star, there it is in the flickering sanctuary light. If you seek the Child in white swaddling clothes, there He is in the snow-white garment of the sacred host. If you seek shepherds and kings, there they are in the simple and the learned who crowd the pews and come to adore. We always have Christmas because we always have Christ in the Mass.

The Christmas season and its merriment die with the dying year, and there is always something melancholy about a year's passing. But here strides in the Christian virtue of hope, reminding us that we have not buried a year — we have planted it, and some day there will be a reaping and a harvesting of its prayers and good deeds. In fact these are the days to ask God for His help in the year ahead. These are the nights, as we say our evening prayers, to ask Him to place under the broad spreading branches of the December dark, that tree whose twinkling bulbs are the distant stars, the four finest gifts that a human being can hope for: a clean conscience, a happy heart, reasonably good health and the courage to cope with any setback or sorrow that the new year may bring.

Knowledge vs. Wisdom

If the incredible Christmas star blazed brightly outside that miserable hovel in Bethlehem, the lamp of learning glowed brilliantly inside, because there were gathered before Madonna and Child the three Wise Men, or, in our terms, the intellectuals, the intelligentsia of their day. But if they had had only learning, they would never have found the Christ. It was not the white light of knowledge in their minds half so much as the red glow of love in their hearts that made them follow the guiding star. When the Almighty broadcasts on His particular wavelength, mere brains alone cannot pick it up. It is good will, humility, virtue, the honest search for truth — these are the outreaching antennae that seem to snatch out of nowhere the call of God.

We live in a day when it is more and more common for a young man or woman to set his or her sights on a college diploma as the magic carpet that will waft one to the highest places. Now, no one finds fault with such planning to make a living; but no one should forget that the main purpose in this world is to attain eternal life. Education is good, and culture is good, but they are not good enough. What benefit is a sheepskin if it hides a wolf? Except that nothing can be hidden from God.

No one should downgrade learning. The Wise Men of Bethlehem were presumably learned in the lore of their times. But the Christian will put first things first. By all means cultivate the mind, but not at the expense of training the will. To have a learned mind and an undisciplined will is tantamount to having a car with a 150-horsepower engine but a faulty steering wheel and undependable brakes. The almost inevitable end is a crashing moral wreck.

In the proper circles you will be welcome if you have the proper prep school accent. (Somebody said that in England the difference between a gentleman and a cockney was the ability to make certain noises.) A smiling exaggeration, no doubt, but it is still true that if you have urbane diction, polished deportment and the right tailor, society will bid you a courtly welcome.

God goes a bit deeper. He is less interested in the social graces of your breeding than in His sanctifying grace in your soul. He is far more concerned with your morals than with your manners. He is not so much interested in how high may be your IQ as in how high are your principles.

My memory goes back to a workman who labored for years on our church property in Boston. I doubt if Dan Lydon ever went beyond the "fourth book" in the schoolroom of some Irish village. But in his pocket was thrust another book, a simple, shaggy prayer book with dog-eared pages. Every morning at the 7:30 Mass (this was long before the liturgy was in English) you could walk down the aisle on your way to the sacristy and see Dan sitting at the end of his favorite pew, with his calloused hands gripping that prayer book as if he were holding a pair of horses.

When he turned a page you could see where the years had left great oily thumbprints. But somehow (it always seemed to me) out of that book and into Dan's soul had gone the unique goodness that characterized him, the gentleness of manner and the strength of conviction, the kindness to all men and the courage in all crosses, the rugged virtue that seemed to breathe from him like the scent of pine needles from an old gnarled fir. Kneeling there in the humblest of working clothes, he was the highest type of God's own gentleman, a Ph.D. from the university of decent living. Across the long centuries he was a spiritual descendant of the Wise Men who had first found wisdom at the feet of Christ.

To the Dan Lydons of this world (and, thank God, they are not a few) religion is not just part of life. Basically it *is* life, at least in the sense that nothing is more important. A thing must be done, or, must not be done, according to how it pleases God or offends Him. To them religion is not just ornamental bric-a-brac on the wall. It is the wall; it is life. To such deeply thinking people, religion has to be all or nothing.

In Dan Lydon's Irish village school, he learned his relation to God in the daily religious instruction. In our country's infancy and well into its adolescence, the only schools were private religious schools. Even the big universities, Harvard and Yale and Princeton and Columbia, had religion written into their very

64

charters. Eventually, however, religion was eliminated from the public schools. Catholics had nothing to do with this; we were then too few to matter, or, in either sense, to count. Reluctantly Horace Mann blue-penciled religion off his curriculum plans, because he despaired of getting any agreement among the predominant Protestant denominations.

From that point on, roughly about a century ago, because religion was removed from the day-to-day teaching of the school, it came to be associated only with Sunday and church. Man's relation to God was no longer a matter of everyday practical living. It became a specialized, separated Sunday luxury, like the traditional chicken dinner.

But if you keep religion inside the stained-glass windows of the church, you also keep it out of the frosted-glass doors of the business office. Take religion out of the factory and you encourage the shoddy product and the quick profit. Take religion out of politics and you encourage bribery and graft. Take religion out of the classroom and you encourage cheating.

After all, if people are going to close the door on religion, and deliberately try to take advantage of their neighbors, there are not enough policemen to keep them honest. George Washington was convinced that "without religion there can be no national morality." Experience shows that when the swirling waters of passion sweep on, things like education and culture and respectability are flung aside like a tissue-paper dam. The average man needs more than responsibility to himself. He needs responsibility to God.

It is true that religious truths, like the soul or grace or heaven or hell, cannot be demonstrated like the multiplication table. You can hardly put the Trinity into a test tube and analyze it. There are mysteries that we accept just on the word of God. On the other hand, if we could fully understand them, we would be as bright as God, a distinction to which few of us pretend.

Many of the truths that God has chosen to reveal are

so mysterious that only He knows how they can be unriddled. This does not mean that those men who have lived by religion with complete dedication were stupid dolts or pathetic morons or weird creatures from humanity's sideshow. On the contrary, they were often glittering minds, incisive thinkers, trailblazing leaders and heroes.

Their names sprinkle the pages of the world's diary: Apostles like Peter and Paul, hermits like Jerome and Anthony, warriors like Louis of France and Don Juan of Austria, explorers like Columbus and Marquette, writers like Thomas Aquinas and Bonaventure, martyrs like Thomas More and Oliver Plunket. Bright men, yes, and brave men too — but above all, believing men!

Charles Kingsley wrote to his daughter, "Be good, my child, and let who will, be clever!" The combination is not impossible. The Wise Men were both learned and devout. They followed the guiding star and they followed God's injunctions.

In the grim crises of human life, when the chips are down and our number seems up, in foxholes and in sickrooms, by the side of open graves and at the mouth of mine shafts, when the dark shadow of tragedy slowly falls, you will find that mere learning and culture and manners and poise and all the rest of civilization's elegant props tend to break down. It is then that the realities of the spirit, like the need of God, come to the fore. Keep them there now. When you establish your priorities, put God and your relation to Him first. Which is just another name for religion. It comes before the three R's, and before the rest of the alphabet too.

A Modern Look at Lent

If a suit of armor in a European museum could lift its visor and take a long clear look back at a medieval Lent, what would it see? By modern standards, perhaps, a narrow gray trail of penance that punished every appetite and turned out a pinched, wan Christian. And yet Perry Mason for the defense would have little difficulty in establishing that for every person who injured his health through excessive penance, there have been hundreds who did more damage to themselves through dissipation and overindulgence.

No question about it, the Lents of yesteryear were stricter in their regulations. Fifty years ago, when we entered the seminary, our Lenten suppers were handed out in carefully calibrated eight-ounce portions. Even up until the end of World War II the breakfast tables in Redemptorist rectories had a scale to weigh your two ounces of dry bread or Graham crackers. One of our old Polish Fathers told me that as a boy in Poland he never saw meat in his home from Ash Wednesday till Holy Saturday.

Regulations may be a matter of degree. Penance is a matter of necessity. In that sense Lent is not connected with history, medieval or modern, but with human nature. Before the bar of conscience an atomic scientist is only a sinner. On his way to splitting the atom he may have fractured a few commandments and therefore, like any medieval monk or merchant, has need of penance. It was Christ, the Man for All Centuries, who voiced the awesome warning: "Unless you do penance, you shall all likewise perish."

What Alpine snobbishness makes the modern man think he is by all odds a better man than the medieval or the ancient? Have we not also our monumental faults? Is it not a world of overproduction and undernourishment? With bombing planes is it not easier to be killed, and with the birth-control pill harder to be born? We may have reached the moon, but we have not come appreciably closer to heaven. True, we have more schools. And more jails. Would that not hint at the possibility of more sin, and therefore the need of more penance?

The modern in his jeans may like Lent even less than his

forebear in his jerkin, but isn't that merely because he is softer? The oxcart has become the Greyhound bus, and the stagecoach a jet. Even a medieval monarch did not enjoy central heating, not to speak of air conditioning. His Majesty's ordinary life-style would constitute considerable inconvenience for a modern handyman. No wonder Lent and our serene comfort are natural enemies.

Along comes a sneaky Ash Wednesday, and all at once it stands in front of us like a sudden stop sign. STOP and DETOUR. The prodding message is to give up something for God. Note this, though, we are not supposed to like the sacrifice. To cuddle up to something painful is against human nature. In any era, Lent will always have to be in the class of those unpleasant but necessary items like a surgeon's scalpel or a dentist's drill or an alarm clock. But, then, who ever said Christianity was supposed to be a velvet, baby-blue, afternoon-tea religion? Has not its central symbol always been the cross?

The meaning of Lent (penance) will be out of date only when sin is out of date. When guilt disappears over the horizon, Lent can follow in its tracks. But not till then. Meanwhile it is good to get this straight: The command to do penance comes from Christ. Lent comes from the Church only as a help to that end.

Ideally we would not need a Lent. Ideally, for that matter, employees would be so absorbed in their work they would never think of glancing at the clock. Ideally, too, soldiers would be eager to be up and doing before reveille. Practically, though, because of human nature, we do have reveille and first sergeants. For the same solid, pragmatic reason we have Lent.

In our modern era the specified restrictions are fewer so the whole Lenten picture is more flexible and fluid. In one way this is harder, because it throws the choosing and the doing of the penance on ourselves. After all, there are only, in the whole six weeks of Lent, two legally prescribed fast days. As the bewildered old lady muttered to me, "Just who does the Pope think he is?"

Apparently he thinks we are no longer spiritual children but mature and responsible adults. He feels thàt by this time in history we realize that the purpose of Lent is not merely to change the menu but to change men and women. And this penance is not something superfluous, a pious extra, like simonizing your halo. It is something coldly and bleakly necessary, like straightening out the bent nail of past sin. Incidentally, it also tones up the moral muscles against tomorrow's temptations.

For this essential reason penance was necessary (and therefore its prodding reminder, Lent) way back in the days when Richard the Lionhearted never doubted that he was the brisk and forward-looking modern. It will be equally necessary when folks in the unpredictable twenty-second century smile at the curious quaintness of the 1970s.

Gadgets change, but not God, and not human nature. Progress, alas, is achieved mostly in the areas of things, not of people. As long as there are people, there will be sin. As long as there is sin, there must be penance. As long as there is need for penance, there must also be need for a Lent to nudge our reluctant souls.

Spring-cleaning

Like many other things in the Church it has changed, but until recently the priest used to cover in his daily breviary the whole one hundred fifty psalms every week. At times that Latin could be bluntly eloquent and frequently stop you in your prayerful tracks.

There was one phrase, for example, *Et scopebam spiritum meum*, meaning, "I set about sweeping out my soul." And in your mind you saw a man standing in the doorway of his spirit, plying an energetic broom and sending up a cloud of swirling gray dust.

Ash Wednesday reminds us that the time has come again for this domestic task in the spiritual realm. The word "Lent," after all, in old English meant "Spring." So what better time to give the house of our soul its own spring-cleaning? Not a popular pastime, to be sure, because poor old human nature much prefers to let sleeping dust lie, or at best sweep it under the rug!

Nobody wants to be reminded of his faults. Everybody wants to stay undisturbed. It takes courage to go down into the cellar of our soul, and search out the trash and the junk that molder in the dark shadows. But we must do it, not in the name of *Good Housekeeping* but in the name of God!

Old grudges, ancient hates, long-ago quarrels with rust on them, age-old jealousies wrapped in cobwebs, perhaps even a hidden habit of serious sin, scarred and ugly and covered with mildew . . . oh, how often we made up our minds we would get rid of it once and for all, but perhaps we never did. If so, then there it still is, and like all the rest it poses a fire hazard, only the hazard here is the fire of hell.

What supreme confidence some of us have! We are so sure that sudden death will not shine its flashlight on our doorbell and murmur, "Yes, this is the place. They don't expect me, but this is the place. The house is an unsightly mess, but this is the place." We dare not judge any man, but on the surface it surely seems that some lives are like garbage scows loaded down to the waterline with presumption. They will have plenty of time, they tell themselves, plenty of time to get ready, plenty of time to prepare, plenty of time to clean house.

The sacraments will be there when they want them. The sacraments will be there, all right, but shall *we* be here? Are they *in our employ* like an attorney or a physician? Is God like a dog to be whistled at when we want Him? Have we but to call, and He comes trotting eagerly to our side? I am afraid we may discover that d-o-g and G-o-d are opposites. The Lord God gives us just so much time, and then *He calls us.*

The sober fact is that if we wait till too late, our house will be past cleaning. Then it is only fit to be condemned and demolished. To put it another way: Some people put off giving up certain pet sins till they are sick or old. But then, is it not the truth that they are not giving up the sin, but rather that the sin is leaving *them*? They had meant to play it bold, and flick at the feet of God the cigarette stub of their last few hours of life. But now they find it drops weakly from their fingers.

Pity those poor souls whose lives have been one long broken promise to walk the repentant trail of the Prodigal Son. They collapsed before they got around to it. Perhaps they never really dared *say*, "When I am good and ready I'll come back to God," but they never thought that God might be ready to call them to account before they had made up their minds to be good. Heaven is not a lottery where luck wins the prizes. Salvation is allotted to those only who have struggled and worked for it. Heaven is not a junkyard of broken-down cars that went to pieces on the road, and had to be towed in. The whole point of heaven is that you have to enter on your own power, your own free will, your own rejection of evil and practice of good.

The trouble is that many who would be repelled and revolted by physical filth can gradually get used to moral evil. This moral evil will not smudge your hands like pitch, nor stain your clean shirt like tar; but it is there and it does stain. Like an invisible atomic fallout it rains down on a soul and defiles it with the vileness of grimy guilt.

Who can vividly portray the awful (and there is no other word) effect of serious sin upon the human soul? Picture a silver fountain, like swaying plumes of tinkling crystal. This is the soul in the state of grace, of God's friendship. Enter serious sin, and before your eyes, you see the fountain gone, and you look down on a sewer of black, slimy, stagnant slop. Or, in a museum, raise your eyes to a masterpiece of art, and one moment later see it splattered with a bucket of mud. More than one saint has solemnly said that if we could see the horrid ugliness of one mortal sin, we should die. We certainly would not want to keep it under our own roof. We surely would clean house quickly!

Sometimes, when people clean house, they are understandably reluctant to toss out this or that. Granted it is rubbish, but they have become attached to it. But this should never be true of moral evil. For here, in getting rid of this, how can we lose? It is true that sin may produce momentary pleasure, but because by its nature it stabs deep into our sensitive conscience, it can never deliver genuine happiness.

Where after all does happiness reside? Not in the palate or the eye or the ear or the flesh — or even in the rich thoughts of the mind or the deep emotions of the heart. Basically, happiness dwells in the depths of a man's soul, in the castle of his conscience. If your conscience is not at peace, even pleasure is restless and uneasy. It is like a luxurious home with a dead skunk under the front porch. Thus it is that the rancid odor of guilt seeps in even into the sinner's so-called good times.

But this is not all. Grant that sin is ugly, grant that it can never bring true happiness, there is something else. The Prodigal Son was a pro in this division and he could put us straight. You know his story. He left his home because temptation in its glamorous silks beckoned him on, always whispering that happiness lay just beyond the next hill. Just another delusion from the Father of Lies!

The Prodigal Son came limping back to his home because his shame disgusted him and his hunger prodded him and his loathsome life had clouded his wide, innocent eyes. All this conditioned him to repentance, but he really made his act of contrition when he saw his aged father come tottering forward to meet him. In that warm, fatherly embrace, the wayward son was sorry for his past, sorry beyond his want and suffering, sorry beyond his humiliating disgrace, heartily sorry because he had hurt and offended this best of fathers. This was perfect contrition, and if we feel that way about our Father, God, we shall feel that way too.

But Lent is more than a clarion call to do a little spring-cleaning in the cellar of our soul, or of plodding back on the saw-dust trail with the Prodigal Son. It is also a plea to do penance for the past — to make amends for our insults against the Almighty.

Many years ago I remember bringing Viaticum to a Carmelite nun. The cloister door opened with a great rattle and clatter of bolts and chains, and four nuns deeply veiled and holding lighted candles softly padded on before me, dolefully chanting the "Miserere." The sickroom was the poorest, barest, most austere room I had ever laid eyes on. Even the cross was bare; there hung from it no figure of Christ. Later I learned that the Carmelite herself was supposed to hang in spirit there, suffering in the place of Jesus.

Ever since then I have wondered: Is the right man on the cross? The cross is atonement for sin, but You, Lord, never committed sin. You never turned Your back on Your heavenly Father. You never stretched out Your hands to welcome sin. Why then should the nails be piercing You? When *we* have done the sinning, why should *You* do the suffering?

It is so easy to *feel* guilty and sorry. Lent is the time to do something about it. Here at home is a soft easy chair and perhaps a color television. Over there in the church there is a hard kneeling bench and the vivid stations of the cross. Shall we translate sentiment into action, or will Lent be just a time when the priest wears purple vestments and the bakeries advertise hot cross buns, but for us the Lenten weeks of March might just as well be January or July?

Do we ever realize that we are the children of martyrs? Maybe we cannot do *much*. We should do *something*.

The Olive Orchard

When we stand on the shore of the Red Sea of our Savior's suffering and brood on how far it stretches, how deep it descends, and how bitter its somber waters, we marvel at *how much* He endured. Any single grim episode is overwhelming. Consider, for example, only the opening event, the first drops of blood that sprinkled a trail that would end red as a sunset on the hill of Calvary.

On that first Holy Thursday night Jesus and His Apostles were coming away from Mass, the first Mass that was also the Last Supper. They plodded through the eastern gate of the city, and soon were filing between the whitewashed tombs that loomed like ghosts along the road. Up above, a near-full Paschal moon gleamed as if it were a large silver plate on a dark mantel, while the far-off stars trailed across the sky in a twisting vine of delicate white buds.

The Apostles took no notice. At that moment their little band was blind to any beauty. Still echoing in their ears was the startling warning of the Master: "Tonight your faith in me will be shaken, for Scripture has it: 'I will strike the shepherd and the sheep of the flock will be dispersed'" (Matthew 26:31). Of course they had all protested their loyalty and their valor, especially Peter. Poor rash, brash, impetuous Peter! He had swept his scornful eye over the rest and cried out to our Lord: "Though all may have their faith in you shaken, mine will never be shaken!" (Matthew 26:33). Jesus, who could look into the future as easily as we look into the next room, gazed levelly into the eyes of Peter and said sadly, "Before the cock crows tonight you will deny me three times" (Matthew 26:34).

Isn't there a little bit of Peter in each of us? How confidently we rely on our moral strength! How sure we are of the great things we will do for God! And yet how many times have we had to bow a blushing head in the confessional, and promise our soul that such and such would never happen again. But it did happen, and it will happen, until we realize that even the best of us cannot be good, unless the Lord gives it; and He will give it only in answer to sincere and almost desperate prayer. The bleak desert of this world's temptations is white with the bleaching bones of those who thought they could cross on their own.

For Christ and His Apostles, the journey from Jerusalem to the lower slope of Mount Olivet took less than a half hour. There they came to a shadowy grove that we generally call the Garden of Gethsemane. Actually it was more an orchard than a garden, with trees rather than flowers. In the main, the trees were olive, and the very name *Gethsemane* means "olive press." It would have been more fitting if it were called winepress, because here the heart of Christ was crushed between fear and sorrow, so that the first crimson drops of the Passion oozed from His pores to stain the bright spring grass.

Of the eleven Apostles on hand (Judas was absent on his traitorous business) our Savior left eight at the entrance of the orchard, and took three with Him deeper into the trees. These were Peter, James and John, selected perhaps because these three had seen him transfigured in glory on Mount Tabor, and so were less likely to be shocked when they saw Him groaning in agony on Mount Olivet. But even these three He now left behind, and pushed farther into the orchard to pray alone.

Christian art has painted this scene often, and always with an awed and mystified brush. Overhead, the silver lacework of the olive leaves; on the ground the great gray rock with Christ kneeling against it like a rugged prie-dieu, and His bearded profile praying, "My Father, if it is possible, let this cup pass me by . . ." (Matthew 26:39). Nothing in all His life confirms more clearly that Christ was like us in all things except sin than does this hour of heartbreak. Mount Calvary might be the crucifixion of His body, but Mount Olivet was the crucifixion of His soul.

Here He experiences what we all have known — the bitterness of a pleading prayer not answered. But He knows that His prayer cannot be answered, else how could the world be redeemed? His head bows in resignation and the trembling lips say, "My Father, . . . your will be done!" (Matthew 26:42). This was not just fatalistic cooperation with the inevitable. It was His deliberate choice. He freely willed, though it meant suffering and death, to atone for the sins of men. Otherwise, no ropes could ever have bound Him to the pillar of the scourging, no nails could have held Him to the cross; only love could hold Him fast.

The Lord, because He was the Lord, did not have to submit to crowning with thorns or carrying of the cross or anything whatever. Voluntarily He endured each thin red trickle, each deep red wound, in order to make reparation for the likes of us. Saint Paul puts it with shattering simplicity when he tells us that Jesus loved us, and delivered Himself up for us. As the fall of man began in the Garden of Eden, the redemption of man began in the Garden of Gethsemane.

"Who takes away the sins of the world." The thought of those sins pressed Him to the earth and induced a bloody sweat. It was as if all the evil of the ages paraded past Him that night in shameful procession. Every crime committed in the history of the world bowed mockingly before Him and hissed: "Hail, Master, I am yours! Atone for *me*!" Dishonesty was there with its bags of ill-gotten gold and its crooked business deals. Drunkenness was there with its silly simper and its slobbering lips. Lust was there with its sliding, leering eye. Murder wiped its dripping red hands on His garment. He must pay the bill for them all.

Had our Savior been a stolid, sluggish soul, it might not have been so bad. There are people (and we have all met them) who are about as sensitive as a heap of soggy leaves. But Jesus Christ was the most perfect person ever made, finely attuned like a concert instrument, and He reacted to every impression with the response of a raw nerve. Imagine Him then, between the deafening chorus of all the sins of the world's yesterdays, and the horrible vision of the morrow's physical tortures, and, hanging over all, the sad knowledge that for many sinners His sufferings would be in vain! The blood that would spurt out in scarlet streams would be flung back into His face in scorn, not only on the hill of Calvary, but on so many other hills and valleys and cities across an ungrateful world.

Is it strange that His human nature winces and groans and trembles? Suddenly He remembers His Apostles, especially the chosen three. With them at least He would find comfort. So He struggles to His feet and starts toward them. But what is this sound He hears? The placid snoring of carefree peasants! What is this sight He sees? Are these the valiant men who offered to die with Him, now fast asleep in the shadows? More in sadness than in anger He asks, "So you could not stay awake with me for even an hour?"

At least the Apostles could argue that as yet they had not received the Holy Spirit. Pentecost had not dawned with its red tongues of fire. Far be it from us to sneer at the snoozing Apostles. We *have* received the Holy Spirit, we *have* been confirmed, we *have* been received into the army of Christ. We are at least privates first class, and we have had our basic training. But what is our service record? Have we never been asleep at our post and let some temptation suddenly overwhelm us? Have we not at times deliberately gone over to the enemy? On what side are we, even at this moment?

It is true that the Apostles then did not die with Christ. But after Pentecost they did die for Christ. He does not ask that much of us. He wants only that we should try to live for Him in purity and honesty and kindness and fidelity. Perhaps if we gaze long enough at His pathetic figure on the television screen of our imagination, sweating blood under the olive trees, that picture may touch our heart, jolt our conscience, and move our weak will to be the kind of person we ought to be: a Christian who really tries to follow Christ!

Holy Thursday: Holy Mass

If the Mass were a stately mansion, the main room would, of course, be the Consecration. Still, it is a curious fact that if we were to enter the church just before the Consecration, we would have "missed Mass," because we were not present for the Offertory. And yet, while the Offertory is necessary to fulfill our obligation, it is not necessary for, and only a preliminary to the sacrifice. One proof of this is that, if the celebrant were to topple over at the altar with a heart attack any time before the Consecration, the sacristan would simply gather up the wafer and the chalice of wine and take them into the vestry. No other priest would have to finish that Mass because in the strictest sense the Mass had not begun.

Up to this point the priest at the altar is only like a violinist who has just finished carefully and lovingly tuning his instrument. Now he is ready for the concert. All that has gone on before — the readings from Scripture, the offering of bread and wine, the washing of the hands — all these are only by way of preparation. We have just passed the foothills of the ceremony and only now approach the Alpine peak of the Consecration.

The congregation knows it. Hitherto a few of the people may have been coughing thoughtlessly, some may have been shifting from knee to knee restlessly, and others leafing through the pages of a missalette listlessly. But now the altar bell sends a silver shiver through the church, as if it were shaking its tiny head and clucking its silvery tongue in warning and rebuke. All at once the whole church holds its collective breath in an expectant hush. We are standing at the very threshold of the Holy of Holies.

At the altar the priest extends his hands over the white-palled chalice, almost like a bishop laying hands on a white-robed seminarian before ordination. But the transformation at the altar goes far beyond that from seminarian to priest. It is the changing of bread and wine into the body and blood of Jesus

Christ. Obviously, only the power of God can accomplish this. Equally obviously, the priest can be only an instrument, an agent, even a puppet.

Herein lies one advantage of the long, flowing, colorful priestly vestments. They minimize the man and emphasize the office. At best all we see in robes of green or purple or scarlet is a distant face and a pair of hands. The person does not matter — only his priesthood does. It makes no difference whether the man at the altar is Father Schneggenberger or Father O'Shaughnessy, whether he is a pink-cheeked curate on his first assignment or a silver-haired veteran of the missions. All that matters is that at this moment he is a priest, standing, as it were, in the sandals of Christ, and reliving word for word and action for action what happened at the Last Supper when the Savior commanded, "Do this in memory of me!"

"The day before he suffered, he took bread and said, 'This is my body.'" Reverently the priest raises the sacred host for the people to adore, and then he himself bends the knee.

"When supper was ended, he took the cup and said, 'This is the cup of my blood.'" Like a man lifting a toast to his Maker, the celebrant raises the golden chalice, replaces it on the altar and genuflects to adore.

But now on the snowy linen lies no longer a piece of bread or a cup of wine, but only their appearance. What is there is Jesus Christ, body and blood, true God and true man.

Of all mysteries this is the most staggering and stupendous. To the incredulous and headshaking non-Catholic who protests, "This is too much; how can you accept it?" there is only one answer: We take God's word for it. We do not claim to understand how it can be, but on God's own word we believe that it is. And we have two strong props to support our belief.

The first is that long before the Last Supper, Jesus had foretold and promised in the town of Capernaum what He would do in Jerusalem on Holy Thursday. He had solemnly declared,

"The bread I will give you is my flesh, for the life of the world" (John 6:51). The reaction then too was skepticism. Scripture says that some of His followers muttered, " 'This sort of talk is hard to endure! How can anyone take it seriously?' ... From this time on, many of his disciples broke away and would not remain in his company any longer" (John 6:51, 66).

So what did Christ do? Nothing. Absolutely nothing. Did He call them back and say, "Look, you misunderstood me. I was speaking poetically, not literally. I really didn't mean it that way at all"? Far from it! He had spoken simply and plainly. They had understood clearly and rightly. Because He had meant what He said, He had no choice but to let the unbelievers go.

The second sturdy prop under our belief is this. Fountains of miracles, by which Christ proved His divine power, now begun to spurt forth after the promise. Our blessed Lord opened blind eyes and deaf ears, straightened twisted limbs and made lepers whole, stilled the stormy sea and drew the dead from their graves. There were even miracles pointing the finger of prophecy toward the Mass, as when He multiplied the bread on the mountaintop, foreshadowing His presence among all the hosts at the communion rail. And the changing of water into wine at Cana subtly anticipated His power to change wine into His own blood.

It was only after this long procession of glittering miracles to establish His almighty power that our Lord fulfilled His promise. It was only on the night before He died that Christ took the bread into His holy hands and said, "This is my body." Could it be said more clearly? Note that He did not say, "This is like my body," or "This is a symbol of my body," or "This is a souvenir of my body," or "This is a memorial of my body," but simply and solely, "This is my body."

And this is how the Apostles and the early Church understood it. Does not Saint Paul ask, "The bread which we break and the chalice which we drink, is it not the flesh and the blood of Jesus Christ?" For fifteen hundred years the whole Christian Church never dreamed of any other meaning. Since then not one jot or iota of scriptural evidence has ever come forward to warrant a different interpretation.

The Scriptures have not changed, but at one period of history it seems that the hearts of men did change. When some of them began to throw over the hard, thorny elements of religion, when they found it too hard to gather around the altar for worship every single Sunday, when they found it too hard to confess their sins to a fellow human being, when they found it too hard to live with one spouse till death did them part, when they found it too hard to acknowledge the Pope as the successor of Peter and head of the whole Church — then they found it too hard also to believe in the Mass. And they turned away from it.

For that matter we Catholics have never found this mystery easy to understand. But understanding a mystery is one thing; accepting it is quite another. Why then do intelligent people believe? For just one towering reason: because we take God's word for it. How many intelligent men have done just that! No one can dodge the solid historical fact that the early saints of the Christian Church all said Mass. Saint Jerome said Mass, and so did Saint Augustine, and Saint Benedict, and Saint Bernard and Saint Thomas Aquinas. No matter whence our Christian forefathers came, they heard Mass. King Alfred heard Mass, and King Richard the Lionhearted heard Mass. Chaucer heard Mass. Clovis and Charlemagne and Joan of Arc heard Mass. Michelangelo and Dante and Rafael heard Mass. Barbarossa heard Mass, and Cervantes and Columbus.

Hilary Belloc used to say, "It is the Mass that matters." Precisely. If the Mass is not true, Christianity is a farce. If Jesus Christ is not present on the altar of the Mass, then for fifteen hundred years the entire Christian religion was only organized idolatry. Not only that. Christ who promised to be with His Church to the end of time (to preserve it from error) is, if we

81

dare form the phrase, a gigantic liar, a fantastic fraud. Every majestic cathedral is nothing but a monumental mockery, and every martyr was a pitiful fool.

But if you go back to the Scriptures, you find it plainly written, "This is my body. . . . This is my blood." And if you go back along the high road of tradition — where the milestones are altar stones leading all the way back to the primitive catacombs — you realize that every Mass (along with carved altars and elegant vestments and all) is only the echo of the divine voice that whispered long ago into the chalice, "Do this in memory of me." Every Mass with its altar cloths is only the setting again of a table that was first set in the upper room on the first Holy Thursday night. Every Mass is but a reprint of the picture that was developed in the darkness that hung over Calvary when that body and blood was sacrificed for the sins of the world.

Because it is founded on Scripture, the Mass that we hear any Sunday goes back to the original Holy Thursday. Through the quiet but awesome miracle of the Mass, the Son of God who had to leave us, has left us a miraculous way by which He can stay among us.

The Joy of Maytime

Maytime is that lovely season when you realize with a pang that God made the country, and then along came man and made the city. In town, where the streets lie like the gray rocky bed of a dried-up river between the looming tenement canyons, about the only clue to the coming of May is in the thermometer. But even in the grimy city we remember parks and suburbs and woodlands and the real May where the youthful year wears a flower in its hair, a song on its lips, joy in its heart, and when a typical day is so glorious it might have fluttered down to earth from the calendar of Eden!

Somehow May sends my memory back forty years to our novitiate in the hills of Maryland. There May was truly Paradise Anticipated. The best hour to greet it was the earliest. We were boomed out of our beds at five by a frantic bell in the lower corridor, a bell that legend said had belonged to a wrecked locomotive. But outdoors (and we would steal outdoors till meditation at 5:30 a.m.) there was an almost cathedral-like hush in the sparkling blue air. On the horizon huge clouds, as often as not a soft violet, hung like curtains on a stage. There was a stirring and a rustling among the leaves like the leaning forward of an expectant audience. Only instead of the houselights of the theater dimming, the dawn came up in a slowly brilliant spread.

To the side a stand of apple trees, laden with white blossoms, bent in the breeze like foam-crested waves. And there were always some eager birds (among them thrushes, orioles and cardinals) trapezing from bough to bough, wearing their gay capes like opera singers and bubbling golden arias. The very air was heavy with fragrance as though nature, like Mary Magdalene, had broken its alabaster jar and spilled its perfume all over the land. And with the balmy air, the bright flowers and the rippling birdsong, you had to throw open the windows of your soul and let the spirit of spring come billowing in across the sill.

Maytime! By the way, do you notice that we never say November time, or August time, or any other month's time? Only Maytime, because May not only has a character, a spirit, a tender beauty all its own, but also seems to be the best time. That is why we Catholics dedicate May, the fairest of months, to Mary, the fairest of creatures. Who doesn't remember the charming hymn we sang in our childhood, and that we catch ourselves humming as adults, " 'Tis the month of our Mother, the Blessed and Beautiful Days''?

And how appropriate it is that May, month of the tender young leaves, the month of promise, should precede the month of June, the month of a rich luxurious foliage, the month of fulfillment! For even thus, May which is the month of Mary, leads to June, the month of the Sacred Heart. The pastel-tinted days of May, as they march along, are like little girls in a Forty Hours procession, strewing their flowers in the path of the oncoming Sacred Heart, the sacred host in the monstrance all gold and burning bright like the June sun!

In Catholic theology Mary exists only for Jesus. On earth her whole vocation was to give Jesus to men as His Mother; in heaven her role is to bring men to Jesus as their Advocate. At the wooden crib at Bethlehem she became His Mother physically; at the wooden cross of Calvary she became our mother spiritually. And if we in America think it only proper to dedicate a special day to our earthly mother, the Church does not count it wrong to set aside a whole month to honor the spiritual mother of us all. And the month the Church chooses is the prettiest of months — gentle, sweet, flower-bright May.

In a sense the coming of May is in the tradition of those legendary artists who work noiselessly all winter long in their secluded chilly attics, but comes the spring and they spread out a gorgeous panorama of pictures, all the way from the left bank of the Seine in Paris to the sidewalks of Greenwich Village in New York. Even so, all through the frozen winter and under the dark soil the Great Artist, God, is silently at work, and then in the spring He flings open His own annual exhibition, all the way from meadows mosaicked with fresh wild flowers to bushes that send out sprays of blossoms like spurting fountains, and even to His miniatures like a velvet rosebud that glows on its stem like a ruby on a scepter.

These are the flowers that in spirit we gather and in love we lay before our Lady and Mother. But mind you, all this time we do not forget, we dare not forget, those other five bloodred roses climbing the trellis of the cross, the crimson wounds of Christ. It is only Christ that we adore, because hanging on the cross He redeemed us as our Savior. His Mother, Mary, we honor, because standing beneath the cross she was faithful to Him to the end.

But as Christ was not just an exceptionally good man, Mary was just not an exceptionally good mother. He was God and could choose His mother, and He chose her for that highest of all human posts. Remember, He did not have to have a mother at all just as in fact He had no earthly father. But He paid the human race the greatest compliment it ever received when He made Mary the Madonna, the Mother of God Himself!

That is the reason why in ages past, emperors were proud to have her image embroidered on their banners, and why sailors sang her hymns over scarlet sunset seas, and why even little children danced with joy around her beribboned Maypole. It goes back to Mary, and the joy throughout Christendom that God had conferred such an honor on one of our own kind. Joy! The best part of the Middle Ages was that somewhere in the middle of them there was a true religious joy, and the concept of the Madonna was near the heart of it.

Have we lost this sense of spiritual joy at some point along the line? We in America have few religious fiestas or real festivals or triumphant processions with music and banners. Do not say that all this external glory would clash with our cold northern temperament. If this is true, how is it that we love a parade? Do we not show our love of country with the blare of bands and the massing of tilted flags and the rhythmic tramp of uniforms?

In patriotism, we let ourselves go. In religion, no. Has the gray breath of Puritanism chilled a natural religious warmth, and silenced the pageantry, the life and the color, the splendor and the music, the spiritual enthusiasm that once marched and sang for sheer joy? Have we forgotten the song of the angels at Bethlehem that rang with gladness, the enthusiastic procession of Palm Sunday that shouted itself hoarse with hosannas, the festive banquet in the parable to welcome the homecoming of the Prodigal Son, the celebration at the wedding feast of Cana whose joy and excitement was fostered and prolonged by Jesus and Mary?

Sadness should be only for sin, the dreary crepe hung on the door of sullen wickedness. Fear is only for those who do not love. But joy is for us who remember that God once chose the all-human Mary to be His Mother at the crib and still chooses to listen to her at the throne. And May is the month we especially remember all this, the month of happiness and hope, the month of the annual miracle of spring's resurrection from the dead, the month when last winter's dry sticks of branches and twigs flutter again with green leaf and bright blossom, the month that assures us that no soul can be so dead but that it can struggle up too, like the seed and the sap, even out of the dirt and the dark to the sunshine of God's grace and the clean beauty of virtue!

So be it. Hearts on high then, for us all! Joy is for the taking. When we bank flowers around our Lady's shrine, when we raise our hymns to her image, when we salute her with her tenderest titles — we are pledging ourselves to serve Almighty God and to honor His holy Mother. But we are doing it with radiant joy, because there is springtime in our souls and Maytime in our hearts!

Did Ever Heart Love More?

If the feasts of the Church were a bright procession of marching banners, the feast of the Sacred Heart would be right up there in the front ranks. In fact, this is a feast of such distinguished stature that it is officially called a solemnity.

Each year it falls on the Friday after Corpus Christi, and by a happy coincidence generally close to the feast of many people's favorite Madonna, Our Mother of Perpetual Help. When we remember how Mary bent so closely over the baby heart of Christ at Bethlehem, and how she stood so near the bleeding heart of Christ on Calvary, it seems only right that her feast should be close to the feast of the Sacred Heart on the calendar of the Church.

After all, while the leaves of nine months were falling from the calendar, these two hearts made a duet of sweet music in one breast. Those were the precious months when the heart of Mary was like a throbbing loom, weaving with scarlet threads the heart of the Savior-to-be.

In those hallowed, intimate days, was not her virginal body the first church of the Nativity, where her holy womb was the tabernacle, and the tiny heart of Jesus the little red sanctuary lamp?

That was before His birth. After it, the picture of Our Mother of Perpetual Help reminds us that He was so often cradled in her soft arms, snuggled close to her heart, two hearts that beat almost as one.

Jesus and Mary, heart to heart! So it was through His helpless babyhood at Bethlehem; so it was in fostering love during His boyhood at Nazareth; so it was while living under the same roof, right up to His public life in Galilee. From that point on, when Jesus had to be about His Father's business, Mary modestly melts into the background. As a matter of record, there are really only two scenes in our Lord's ministry where the Gospel paints Mary prominently into the picture.

But notice this. In each incident, Mary is not only at the side of Christ, but in each case His heart opens. The first time was a wedding. The second was a wake. The first scene was Cana; the second Calvary. At the first, Mary whispered to Jesus the plight of the bride and groom, and at her prayer His sympathetic heart opened and He gave them sparkling red wine. On the second occasion, Mary was praying secretly for us all, and again His heart was opened, this time by a soldier's lance, and He gave the world the last of His red, saving blood.

It is comforting to realize that the same heart of Christ,

through the miracle of the Blessed Sacrament, is still with us today; and in most churches there stands near the tabernacle an image of Mary. On that Good Friday so long ago the Roman soldier ran his lance into the body of Christ, pale as a marble tabernacle, and blood leaped out like red rain. On the Friday of the feast of the Sacred Heart, a priest runs his key into the altar tabernacle, and the sacred hosts of Holy Communion begin to fall on uplifted tongues like flakes of snow.

Generally speaking, the heart is a symbol of love. It took a great deal of love for God to become a baby within the four rough boards of a crib. It took even more love to hang as a corpse on the two splintery planks of the cross. But it took the most love of all to take the form of bread in the tabernacle. That is why we know that the love of our Lord is not something that stopped at Bethlehem or Calvary. It is with us still, even greater than before.

In the beginning, a fire burns in the forge with bright red flames, but as the heat grows fiercer, the fire glows white-hot. So it was with Jesus. When He was lifted up on the cross, His love for us burned red in His dripping blood; but when He is lifted up in the host, His love burns white, because it takes more love to take the form of bread than that of a man.

On Calvary, Jesus proved He loved us enough to die for us. In every tabernacle He proves He loves us enough to live among us.

That helmeted Roman centurion who plunged his spear into the side of the Savior thought he was only going about his official business: making sure that the victim was, beyond any doubt, dead. He did not dream that God was using him (as He had used Caesar Augustus to announce the census, and Pontius Pilate to order the cross) to give us the devotion of the Sacred Heart.

Since then, that heart has been forever open, and every sinner has a refuge to which he can flee. How senseless to try to run away from guilt when the long arm of God can reach to the ends of the earth! But if the sinner comes close, very close, God cannot strike, but only embrace.

Jesus said, "Learn of me, for I am meek and humble of heart." Meek and humble, and merciful too! Above all, merciful!

November Is Remember

On a sparkling day in May in the early 1920s a half-dozen of us Redemptorist seminarians were visiting Niagara Falls on our way home from the minor seminary. We were standing behind an iron rail so close to the falls that you could almost lean over and touch the bright, roaring water. But what distracted us from the wonder of this thundering cataract was a young workman in paint-stained overalls who sat on a nearby bench and held his head in his hands and shook with sobs.

Two of us sauntered over to him. We were afraid that he might be literally on the brink of suicide. It turned out that death had already been there. In his broken English, and with a broken voice, he told us that about an hour ago he and his best friend had been painting the railing a little farther below. His friend had slipped. He heard the scream and saw his friend go hurtling through the air, drop into the foaming rapids and disappear. The police had come, boats had been notified, but there was no trace of the man. Now this poor crying fellow was waiting for the police to come back, and then he would have to go to his friend's home and break the news. "His wife is even now putting the dishes on the table for his supper. And I must tell her he will not be home for supper. He will not be home ever."

Since then every one of our little group, now long since priests, has often had that same melancholy mission, breaking the news of death. Is there any assignment that is tougher? Teenagers sometimes think that a policeman buttons his blue serge coat over a heart of granite; but I have known a patrolman to walk back and forth seven or eight times in front of a house before he summoned the courage to ring the bell and go in with his cap in his hand and practically gulp out the bad news.

Sometimes that news is heard with an unbelieving stare, sometimes with a heartrending, hysterical scream. But human nature is a strange composition, and time is a tender bandage, and the world is a welter of pressing day-by-day duties, so that eventually the dead one becomes only a name on a polished headstone or a picture on a polished piano. So soon do people fade away. Out of sight, out of mind. That is why the Church sets aside one month each year to remind us ever so gently of those we have loved and lost and have all but forgotten. November is remember.

Not merely remember, of course. Remember and help. But can the deceased be helped? If they cannot, why does the Scripture tell us that Judas Maccabeus, the valiant Jewish captain, sent twelve thousand pieces of silver to the temple to have sacrifices offered for the sins of the soldiers who had just fallen in battle? If there were no dead who needed help, if there are no dead who could be helped, then these words of Scripture would be futile. And Scripture is never futile.

Further, if we look at the situation under the strong white light of logic (without invoking Revelation) there must be many of us who, while not bad enough for the red fires of hell, are not quite good enough to have the red carpet of heaven rolled out for us and be immediately escorted into glory. For such (and there are a great many of us) who have sinned and been forgiven but have not done much penance — for such individuals, does it not seem reasonable that there should be an intermediate place, a kind of halfway house where souls are purified before they are admitted into the presence of the all-pure God?

This intermediate place between heaven and hell is called purgatory. The very word "purgatory" in its Latin origin means "a place of purging or cleansing." But purgatory is of interest to the living only because we can deliver our loved ones from it. Our prayers and good works can pay the fine and liberate the prisoners.

In this connection, the average wake is likely to be not only a scene of loss but also of remorse. Only when the leaves die, and the tree stretches out its gaunt black branches, can you see the nests of summertime. So too it is only with the death of a parent that unpleasant incidents of the past, like snubs and slights and quarrels and sharp remarks, stand out on the tree of memory. How often a son or daughter confides with trembling lips to a priest standing next to the coffin, "I wanted my mother to know how much I loved her, but somehow I never got around to it." Or, "I wanted my father to know how much he meant to me, but he is dead now, and I never told him." It is a feeling like rushing down to the train with a farewell gift and getting there just as the train pulls out, except that the black train of death speeds away into the unreachable hereafter.

But that is precisely why November should be a month of tender consolation to us all. Perhaps you always wanted to give your deceased parents some kind of worthwhile trip, a truly grand vacation. Now you may be able to give them the finest trip ever, to send them on an endless, glorious vacation, heaven! You can help them take the biggest step any human being ever takes, that ecstatic step backward from November second to November first, from the gloom of purgatory and All Souls, to the glory of heaven and All Saints!

If we have treated our dear ones too coldly, too sharply, too impatiently, when they were alive, and this memory haunts us as the ghost in armor haunted Hamlet, perhaps our solution is to recall another impressive figure in armor: Goliath. When that glittering giant came striding toward David, a young stripling of perhaps sixteen, it must have seemed like the Eiffel Tower lurching toward him on stilts. And all David had to defend himself with was his slingshot, a few smooth stones from the brook, and the power of God. The power of God! It sent the slingshot whirling, sent the stone whizzing, sent the giant toppling over like a chimney. Then David knelt by the unconscious form, tugged at the huge sword, and finished Goliath off. Who doubts but that he then wiped off the sword and brought it to his tent radiantly clean?

Years later a jealous King Saul decided to have David murdered. Then, when David was fleeing from the king's agents, hungry and without a weapon, he came upon Ahimelech, the priest of the temple at Nob. For food the priest gave him the temple bread. When David asked for a weapon, he pointed to a long sword carefully wrapped in silk near the altar. Ahimelech said, "There is no sword here except that one." David unwrapped the gleaming blade and recognized the sword of Goliath. He hefted it joyfully in his great manly grip. "There is no other sword like this," David said and took it with him.

Little stones and big sword. These were David's weapons and they can be ours too. Weapons to storm purgatory and release the captives. The little stones are the beads of our rosary. How richly indulgenced is every recital of the beads! October is the month dedicated to the rosary, but November is the month in which the beads hang like a key at our Lady's sash. If we say the rosary, Mary can use it to open purgatory and lead our loved ones to happiness in heaven.

The big sword is the one thrust into the hillcrest of Calvary. At least it is shaped like a sword. It goes up and down, over and across like a sword. It is spattered with blood like a sword. This sword is the cross of Christ. But as David found his sword clean and brilliant in the temple, we have in any Catholic church the sacrifice of the cross, bloodless and brilliant in the Holy Mass. During the month of November we should hear Mass for our dear deceased, and also have Masses said for them.

If any of a cynically suspicious mind should think, "Naturally he would recommend having Masses said for the deceased; the priesthood is his profession," let me answer merely this: As for you, do unto others who are dead, as you would have them do unto you. But as for me, when I am dead, leave at my casket only spiritual bouquets, because far more than a mass of perishable flowers I treasure the imperishable flower of the Mass. Imperishable because its merits reach right into eternity!

Eucharist Means Thanksgiving

When modern man discovered penicillin or X rays or radar, it is doubtful if any group got down on its knees to thank God, but about three hundred fifty years ago a band of daring spirits gave thanks to the Almighty just for surviving one brutal winter. There they were, with the wide gray ocean lashing behind them and a rugged, hostile wilderness frowning before them, and they themselves clinging to the edge of a new continent like swimmers on a huge rock — and yet in their frantic struggle for sheer existence they set apart a day dedicated just to murmur "Thank You!" to God.

So the Pilgrims inaugurated Thanksgiving Day. George Washington first officially proclaimed it. Abraham Lincoln, after it had lapsed, revived it during the Civil War. (During war and sickness we tend to think of God.) Franklin Roosevelt pushed it back a week. Congress restored it to its old spot as the last Thursday in November. In New England, where it originated, they treasure it the most fondly and celebrate it the most faithfully.

This is one holiday where the accent of the festival falls on the food, as at Christmas it falls on the gifts, and at Easter on the clothes. That is why we speak of Christmas presents, the Easter fashion parade, but the Thanksgiving dinner. If Thanksgiving were a book, the table of contents would be the contents of the table. It is the time when thousands of housewives talk turkey to the manager of the supermarket — turkey and celery and cranberry sauce.

It is a grim thought (and perhaps only a grasshopper mind would leap to it) that just before he goes to his death a condemned prisoner is allowed to order as rich and varied a meal as he wishes. This, in turn, recalls a very special last meal in an upper room in Jerusalem when only One knew it was to be His last. When He tried to tell His Apostles that He was going to the Father, they could not comprehend. But He knew that on the morrow He would die, so He made that final repast the most celebrated banquet in history, His Last Supper, their first Communion, the institution of the Holy Eucharist.

What a lumbering, pondering phrase that is, institution of the Holy Eucharist! But Eucharist is only the Greek word for "gratitude" or "giving thanks." In that sense is not the Mass the forerunner of Thanksgiving? It was on that hallowed night (as the Scripture says) that our Lord, raising His eyes to heaven, *gave thanks.* Then He broke the bread. The ancient Jews did not cut bread; they broke it. Hence the phrase, "to break bread" with someone. But when it happens in the Mass, it is not just a representation of the Last Supper; it is a re-presentation of it.

Even more than Thanksgiving Day, the Mass is part of a long, noble tradition. The first Mass was offered in Jerusalem, almost twenty centuries ago. Saint Paul celebrated Mass (the Lord's Supper, the breaking of the bread) on the third floor of a crowded dwelling in Troy. When we come up to receive Communion, it might impress us more if we remembered that we are at the end of a long, long line that reaches back to the catacombs and to the early martyrs, those heroes and heroines who received the bread of life in their mouths before they were ground by the teeth of lions in the amphitheater. For us who are called to be only heroes and heroines of the humdrum, the sacred host is our source of strength and courage too.

If Thanksgiving Day recalls why the Pilgrims gave thanks, the Mass reminds us that we have far greater reason to be grateful. But it is not so much the bread as it is the chalice that vividly frames our debt to God. When the priest stands before the altar in the footprints of Christ, obeying the injunction of Christ ("Do this in memory of me") and repeating the very words of Christ, he says, "This is the cup of my blood. It will be shed for you and for all men that sins may be forgiven."

Then and there, in that chalice, is the blood that spurted from the slashing whips at the scourging, the blood that crusted with crimson the nailheads at the crucifixion, the blood that glowed like rosebuds amid the thorns of His bristling crown, the blood that fell in huge drops like precious coins to pay for our sins. When that chalice is lifted up at the Mass, we realize with a start and a pang how much we have to be thankful for, in a Savior who suffered so much that we might enter into eternal joy.

On the first Thanksgiving Day red Indians and white settlers sat down together at the same rough board near the field where brown cornstalks stood like the stacked rifles of peace. The Mass too is the banquet of friendship, because no man would dare approach it for Communion if animosity exists between him and his fellowman. This is one reason why the Our Father precedes Holy Communion with its incisive prayer: "Forgive us . . . as we forgive . . . " — meaning that if *we* do not forgive, we know *He* will not forgive. In the more ceremonial Masses, like a Solemn Mass or a Concelebrated Mass, there is a living tableau of this forgiveness and friendship as the priests go through a ritual embrace known as the kiss of peace. In most churches some form of this, usually a handshake, goes rippling along the pews and through the whole church.

For many, Thanksgiving Day is an occasion for joyful reunions, and so is, or so should be, the Mass. It is heartwarming to see the faithful in little villages or tiny towns cluster around the church after Sunday Mass, chatting cheerfully, exchanging warm

95

greetings, smiling to this one, nodding to that one, before they go their separate ways to their often distant homes. In the swarming parishes of large cities, there is not much of this. Here we pass like ships in the night. But at least when we march to the altar, we can remember that we are members of the same household of the faith, going to the common table of the communion rail, brothers and sisters of the one spiritual family.

Some devout people, incidentally, are disturbed and even a bit shocked that the present Mass ends so abruptly and sends them out into the street so soon after Communion. The old ritual had its Last Gospel, three Hail Marys, Hail Holy Queen, prayers to Saint Michael, to the Sacred Heart, and often the Divine Praises. In those days, the Mass tapered off more slowly and the extra prayers were a way of thanking God for coming into our hearts. There is no objection, of course, if anyone wishes to remain after the recessional and say some private prayers of thanks. But perhaps the Church wishes to emphasize that we thank God best for His goodness to us by going out and being good to our fellowman. If at Holy Communion our heart is like a chalice brimming with the presence of Christ, its overflow should pour out upon our neighbor. If like Moses we come down from the mountaintop with our face aflame from the nearness of God, the radiance should shine out on all we meet. The Mass is not just part of the day, or the start of the day. It is the heart of the day, and like a heart it should pump, not blood, but blessing into our every action.

To sum up: Because the Mass is the living echo of the most memorable banquet in history, because the altar is our spiritual family table (festal with twinkling lights and gay flowers), because "Eucharist" is only the Greek word for giving thanks, because turkey ranks infinitely below the Lamb of God (that snow-white host), should we not begin Thanksgiving Day by giving thanks *at Mass*? If we do, we thank God as He wants to be thanked: through Jesus Christ, His Son, our Lord.

sprinkles
of holy water

"The One You Love . . ."

In one sense you might call it a ghost story, even a Holy Ghost story, because it comes right out of the pages of Scripture. Therefore, it is no mere spooky yarn but a solid and solemn truth. And so that we shall never forget it, its thrilling message is chanted over the casket in the middle aisle at every Requiem Mass.

The scene was a tiny village, perched like Hummel figurines dotting a shelf, on the lowest slope of Mount Olivet. It was called Bethany and (unlike Bethlehem which achieved fame through a cradle) it won immortality through a grave. To this day the Arabs round about call the place with straight simplicity, *Lazarus.*

Lazarus lived there with his sisters, Martha and Mary. It was a little family so close to Jesus that He regarded Bethany more than any place except Nazareth as His home. That is why the message that Jesus received from Martha and Mary when He was on the other side of the river Jordan needed no name to identify the subject. It said merely, "The one you love is sick."

Was there ever a more discreet and delicate prayer? Here was no demanding, no pressure, no insistence. The two sisters just presented the situation and left everything to the Lord. Their message was a close relative of the prayer of His Mother at Cana who had said only, "They have no wine." Judging from both results, it is the kind of prayer that Jesus likes to hear — and to answer.

But not immediately, and at least in the case of Lazarus we can see why. It had taken the messenger two days to reach our Savior in Peraea, but Jesus still lingered there two days more. He did not want to heal a sick Lazarus but to raise a dead one.

When Jesus finally did propose to the Apostles, "Let us go up to Bethany," they turned pale. Peraea was comparatively safe, but Bethany was the threshold of Jerusalem. This was the center of the enemy's camp, the headquarters of the scribes and Pharisees, the site of the temple where so recently they had tried to stone Him to death. Patiently He explained to them: "Lazarus is dead. I am glad for your sakes that I was not there. It will help you to believe. Let us go!"

There was a pause, a kind of cowardly silence, but out of it came the voice of one Apostle, Thomas the Twin: "Let us go up and die with Him!" Poor Thomas, who has gone down in history as the doubter, is rarely remembered for this. But he has at least survived in a reverent way, for most of us, whenever we see the sacred host lifted on high, silently send up his awesome act of adoration after the Resurrection: "My Lord and my God!"

Now followed two days of dusty uphill travel, and when the group came near the house of Lazarus, Martha ran out first to meet them. After all, she was the practical sister and had probably dried her tears and was already dealing with necessary household details while the mystical Mary swooned away in melting grief. In fact, Martha's first words to Christ (as John records them in Chapter 11 of his Gospel) are so practical that they shock us. It is nothing else but a blunt reproach: "If you had been here, my brother would not have died!" But all at once her heart goes on its knees, and she whispers, "But I know that, even now, whatever you ask of God, he will grant you."

Still, Martha does not come out plainly and ask for the most impossible of miracles, the one that would be the most spectacular in all His public life. Instead it is Jesus who reassures her: "Your brother will rise again!" Here Martha misunderstands and reluctantly admits: "I know he will rise again at the resurrection on the last day."

Then with the simple majesty of truth Jesus reminds her: "I am the resurrection and the life. ... Do you believe this?" Her reply was, "Yes, Lord, I have come to believe that you are the Messiah, the Son of God: he who is to come into the world." Over how many open graves, in how many cemeteries, in how many centuries to come, would those words echo again and again: "I am the resurrection and the life"?

But now our Lord merely asked, "Where is your sister?" At that Martha went running back to the house and soon Mary came hurrying out, and after her a whole troop of mourners, because in old Judea they mourned for a week, and whenever a new visitor arrived to express his sympathy the weird wailing started all over again. Mary fell at His feet, weeping, but Jesus only asked: "Where have you laid him?" "Lord," she answered, "come and see." And the whole motley crowd shuffled down the hillside to the tomb. As far as they were concerned, they were only paying a visit of respect to a grave. Some of them were even critical and mumbled, "He opened the eyes of the blind man, could he not have prevented this man's death?" They conceded His ability to cure. They never even considered the possibility of a resurrection.

The tomb, like most graves in Judea, was cut out of a limestone hill. It was like a cave that began on the level and then dropped a couple of feet beneath the road level. The body was lowered down there, and then a huge stone was rolled against the entrance. This was sealed up and whitewashed to show that it was a tomb and therefore a sacred spot.

Now, when our Savior saw the tomb, He suddenly began

to weep. There are only two occasions in the Scriptures when Christ shed tears, once when He gazed down upon the city of Jerusalem and prophesied its ruin, and the other when He came face to face with the grave of his friend Lazarus. Many a strong man has shed silent tears in a cemetery. Call it what you will, grief or pity or compassion, it is a universal human emotion, perhaps the center note of the keyboard of the human heart, and Jesus, who was human as well as divine, throbbed at its touch.

But a few moments later, as when a gray cloud drifts past a majestic mountain peak, His serenity returned. "Take away the stone!" He commanded. In the crowd there was a moment of whispering indecision, but someone, maybe a farmer with a mattock, began to hack away and break the seal. Others gruntingly pushed back the heavy stone. Then Martha, always the practical one, remembered. It was all very well for Jesus to wish to see for the last time the body of His friend, but what sight, or even what smell would they uncover? It was the spring of the year, it was a hot country, there was no embalming. It was better that Jesus remember Lazarus as he had been. So Martha bluntly blurted out, "Lord, it has been four days now; surely there will be a stench."

But Christ had not come to view a corpse. He stood before the now open tomb and in ringing tones commanded, "Lazarus, come out!"

It was a breathless, awesome moment. People pushed, necks strained, eyes bulged. What would happen? There appeared at the entrance something white, something wrapped in linen, with a napkin half covering its face, something stumbling in its shroud, an upright risen corpse! The murmuring crowd was stunned to silence. They stared wide-eyed with astonishment. Martha and Mary gasped, just one breath away from a scream of joy. Only Jesus was in perfect control. Quietly He pointed to the man four days dead. "Unbind him," He said, "and let him go."

Three times in His lifetime our blessed Lord knocked at the cold door of death. Once He did it for a widowed mother in the town of Naim, once for a brokenhearted father called Jairus, and now in behalf of two sisters at Bethany. This last was without doubt the most dramatic miracle in our Lord's life. In fact, Lazarus alive was so embarrassing to the Pharisees that they plotted to kill him. On the other hand, it was chiefly because of the raising of Lazarus that the common people shortly afterward led Jesus from Bethany into Jerusalem waving palms and shouting hosannas. They little knew that He was marching toward another tomb and the most incredible miracle of all.

The very foundations of the Church are laid in the open graves of these miracles. These dead were the star witnesses to the living God. Lazarus is as much a monument to the faith as Saint Peter or Saint Paul.

But perhaps most pertinent to us in the whole episode is that prayer of the two sisters, a prayer as vivid and outstanding as a flag flying over a fort: "The one you love is sick." It is a prayer to say, a message to send when we are sick with sin, even decaying in a tomb of corruption. The fact is that God still loves us, even then. The wonder is that He can raise us up, even if the sickness of the soul is mortal. Even though a man should fall so low that his feet touch hell, our blessed Lord cannot resist that compelling prayer: "The one you love is sick." It is the resurrection of a soul.

Cremation

Some of us recall when in the long, long ago "Cremo" was advertised as America's favorite five-cent cigar. Long before that, *cremo* was a quiet little Latin verb meaning, "I burn." Nowadays it is buried in the word "cremation," the term that designates the disposing of "the remains" by fire. In the future this residue may be referred to as "the cremains." To one who has never seen the process it suggests a Viking funeral with a thermostat.

At any rate that shrill coterie which likes to linger over cocktails gloating over the changes in the once-unchanging Church (without realizing that these changes touch only the incidentals and not the essentials) now have a brand-new alley to bowl on. And admittedly some of us deep-dyed conservatives will have to adjust.

I can remember years ago, whenever the inquiry about cremation used to pop out of the audience question box, I would give it the shrugging swerve, because I was not that familiar with cremation. But Rome has spoken. Comparatively recent decrees (1963 and 1969), though little publicized, have executed an abrupt turn (not perhaps one hundred eighty degrees) but at least a significant one. And we must turn too.

Till these recent decrees the law was all contained in Canon 1240 (and the quoting of a canon rather than a commandment or the creed should be a tip-off that the change is only a matter of Church regulation), which forbade Christian burial to anyone who wished to be cremated. To such the pastor had to forbid the last sacraments, Funeral Mass and Christian burial.

The new legislation allows all these to any Catholic who opts for cremation, as long as he does so with no defiance of God or denial of immortality. This right attitude is to be presumed. No permission is required for cremation.

To go back a bit. In defense of the Church, Rome never condemned cremation merely on the grounds that while the Church was old-fashioned and conservative, cremation was progressive and modern. Modern? Cremation is about as modern as the Stone Age ax. Cremation was old before the Roman Empire was young, and before the Church was even born. Archaeologists trace it back at least to the pre-Canaanites who lit their funeral fires four thousand years before Christ.

Even civil authority countenanced cremation in Western

society only in the latter half of the nineteenth century. But just about that time a spurt of atheism also promoted cremation as a kind of nose-thumbing farewell to God. Cremation came along as a concrete denial of the hereafter, a smart rebuttal to all this nonsense about immortality. "Okay, God," it said. "You want to punish me for the sins of my life? Well, then punish this!" And poor God was left with only a little gray fluff in an oversize ashtray.

That gesture was not only atheism, it was also idiocy. It displays a naive ignorance of the grim facts of death and deterioration. Anyone who has ever witnessed the transfer of bodies from one cemetery to another is vividly aware that the only difference between the result of interment and cremation is that in the one you end up with a handful of powdery brown, and in the other a handful of sifting gray. Basically, brother, they are both dust, just filtering dust.

Does anyone think that cremation will startle God? His holy word, contained in the Scriptures, bristles with allusions to the disintegration of man's body into dust. Surprised He is not, nor frustrated either. Will cremation prevent the resurrection? Surely it is a lesser achievement to reassemble man out of something, no matter how little, even a puff of ashes, than to make him out of nothing from the very beginning. At least with the dust (of cremation or burial) God has a head start that He did not have in creation. It all goes back to the kind of God you believe in. And if you do not believe in the biggest (the Creator!) then you would do better to forget it.

At any rate, the Church originally opposed cremation because it was associated with atheism and the denial of a life to come. But nowadays these postures of unbelief are no longer the trademark of cremation. So the Church has withdrawn its objections. Never did the Church preach that cremation was intrinsically evil. Proof of this lies in the fact that whenever the public good warranted it, the Church allowed cremation, as in times of plagues, earthquakes and the like. As a matter of fact, in certain countries, like Japan, where cremation was woven into the local culture, the Church always sanctioned it — as long as there was not implied an insult to God or a profanation of the body.

Today in the United States three factors may tend to foster cremation. The first is the saturation of the city cemeteries. True, as yet signs do not hang on cemetery gates advising NO VACAN-CIES, but it may not be far away. A few years ago I buried a brother-in-law who died in Bay Ridge, Brooklyn, my boyhood home. Fortunately there existed a small family plot in Holy Cross Cemetery, Flatbush. Otherwise, the undertaker solemnly said, the funeral cortege would have to drive seventy long miles to the nearest available Catholic cemetery on Long Island. God's acre should never be that far away!

After vicinity comes economy. Cremation naturally eliminates the need of a grave, a fragment of real estate that can be quite expensive, plus opening it for a burial. On the other hand, if you wish to preserve the ashes from cremation in an urn, and enshrine them in a crematorium niche, this can also make a significant inroad into your insurance. However, as cremation gets going, it is quite possible that the casket will become far simpler, on the realistic grounds that after a day or two of use it will be consumed by fire anyway.

At the moment, may we interject that many people buy much too expensive caskets anyway, either under a false sense of duty to the deceased, or from a pale fear of not keeping up even with the dead Joneses. For many survivors, death means also debt.

The third advantage of cremation is the prevention of possible epidemics arising from the burial of infected bodies. However, this danger is rather less than you might suppose. The reason is a dramatic antibiotic that was never developed in a lab but rather scooped from a grave. Just ten years after Fleming discovered penicillin, a man named Dubos came up with the second antibiotic. In his experiment he first contaminated some soil with pathogenic or harmful bacteria. Then he found to his amazement that the soil in self-defense had developed other bacteria to consume the invader. This neutralizing agent, eventually synthesized as tyrocidine, has apparently always risen around cemeteries like an invisible antibiotic wall to prevent pestilence.

Nevertheless, even though cremation seems more hygienic, more economical and more accessible than a distant burial place, the Church still favors traditional interment "under the wide and starry sky." The Church's spirit is still the spirit of the Victorian poet who sang, "Green be the turf above thee, friend of my boyhood days!" Or like Robert Louis Stevenson's old Scotch gardener, who had given his life to the growing of roses, and who at the last was laid among them, so that "the roses still took their life from him, only in a new and nearer way."

Grave or grill, the important matter is not the disposal of the dead body but the destination of the living soul. For the consolation of the bereaved the obsequies at a cremation are the same as at an interment. There is the Funeral Mass in the church, and the final prayers at the crematorium. Dust or ashes mark the melancholy end of the body. There is no end to an immortal soul.

Ghost Town

Every now and then in the Colorado hills a stranger may see a mirage, wrought not by wavering heat but by slow, eroding time. It looks like a town in the distance, but when he gets there, he sees it is only a ghost. Once it was a booming, bustling community. Now its few empty streets lead nowhere. The stray tourist stands on the railroad track and feels the weeds rustle around his knees. He looks up at the faded storefronts with their hitching posts (the parking meters of the Old West) and realizes that these posts have not been touched by a horse's reins in seventy-five years. What few weather-beaten houses remain are tilting weirdly in the wind, and the saloon seems to be swaying as if it were drunk itself. Here was the honky-tonk "palace" of the town, where the piano jangled and the patrons wrangled, and most of them were filled with liquor and a few with lead; but everything now is silent except when some crumbling timber comes tumbling down.

They will tell you that it is the dry air that embalms everything, so that you have a mummy of a frontier town, a backwoods village of death. The death certificate is written in the big holes in the hills, the gold mines that gave out. After that, life went out of the place, like blood from a gravely wounded man. The result is that, though from a distance it may fool you, seen close up the place is a corpse. It is only a ghost town.

How many of us, I wonder, look like that to God? On second thought, none, because God sees us immediately as we truly are. Better rephrase the question. How do we look to one another? We stand next to a man in the subway, or sit next to him at a coffee-shop counter, and to us he is just another person who breathes and talks and walks and is vibrantly alive. But to God, who sees him close up, who sees into his heart, his conscience, his soul, this man's soul may be only a ghost town, nothing inside but spiritual desolation and moral decay. A life of serious sin, unrepented and unconfessed, has turned him into what Christ called a whited sepulcher, a beautiful exterior but within only corruption and decay.

Ever since Vatican II, Catholic pulpits and Catholic papers have been ringing with high-sounding words like *encounter* and *involvement, dialogue* and *identity crisis, fulfillment* and *witness* and *ecumenism*, and all the impressive rest, but (or haven't you noticed?) we hear less and less of that little word, *sin*. Admittedly, it is not a pleasant word, not a popular word — but it is a necessary word, a warning word. Sin is the only thing in this wide world that can make a man's life a total failure, the only thing on all this earth that can keep him out of heaven.

Consider, of all things, a pallbearer. See him in his sedate suit, solemnly wheeling the casket down the church aisle. Is he not the very image of upright and honorable dignity? But reflect. If that pallbearer is in serious sin, then God sees him as even deader than the corpse. The corpse is only an empty, abandoned house, but the soul of the pallbearer is a house with a decaying corpse on the floor, crawling with the maggots of corruption. You think that this is too vivid an image? On the contrary, grave sin is so horrible in the eye of heaven that any merely earthly comparison has to be anemic.

Why? Because if we commit serious sin, we are really telling God to mind His own business! We will do what we jolly well please, let Him like it or not. We practically say we do not care a whit if God in His power created us, and in His mercy redeemed us; we shrug it all off. We fling His precious blood back into His face. Through His commandments He has told us what we should do, but by our life we tell Him where He can go.

This, mind you, is puny man speaking to the immortal Almighty God, because actions do speak louder than words. It is the pebble challenging the mountain. It is the ant standing on the railroad track, waving its antennae and defying the onrushing locomotive.

No wonder the devil rejoices at every serious sin. "Your Son," he can say to God, "died for this person. Yet this person serves me. I did nothing for him, but he listens to me. I offer him eventually only hell, but he stays with me." Of course it is a lie, for the devil is the Father of Lies. Still, the devil does promise something. He promises to satisfy people's passions. To one man's wounded pride he promises sweet crushing revenge. To another's hot lust he offers a menu of drooling sexual sin. To another's avarice he guarantees money, quick, easy and sure.

The worst of it is that so often the devil seems to produce. Smug, smiling, content, the sinner goes his way, while the steadfast, struggling Christian plods a rocky path. Then is the time to remember that our Lord never said that virtue would be rewarded on this earth. On three of four occasions He warned of the exact opposite. Recall that at Bethlehem Jesus was not there in the inn with its boisterous glee and its sensual pleasures. He was in the cave with its loneliness and its cold. On the first Good Friday, He was not in Jerusalem with the happy holiday throngs preparing for Passover. He was hanging on a gibbet outside the city walls. But Bethlehem and Calvary were like two huge hands reaching up to pry open the gates of heaven that had been closed by the rebellion of original sin.

Now that these gates are open, does it not behoove us to mount the stairs to them, even if we have to trample our passions in the process? And we *can* climb as long as we hold on to the banisters or the guardrails, the grace of God.

And if we stumble and fall? Then we struggle to our feet and rise! We go on! Here the important thing is a deep-down determination to serve God, the compass needle of our life always pointing north, a permanent dedication to right and not wrong. Once we have made up our mind to serve God and not our passions, then the past does not matter. It is only the present that counts.

When I was a very young priest I used to wonder how one could reconcile the justice of God with the case of a man who had led a spotless life until right before the end, when he committed one mortal sin and died in that sad state.

With so much going for him on the credit side of the ledger, and so little against him on the debit side, would such a man be condemned to hell? Ask the formal theologians (those of my naive seminary days who docilely trudged in the footprints of Thomas Aquinas, and not the later breed who opt for the "fundamental option") and you got a reluctant, "I'm sorry. Yes."

Only God, to be sure, knows. But I recall reading somewhere a quasi-parallel case, where a much-decorated British regiment in India revolted on the eve of its departure for England and shot its officers. That last-minute mutiny wiped out all its glorious record and branded it *traitor*.

Call it, if you will, a facile comparison and a proof that does not prove. As I grew older I came to accept a much simpler solution, namely that this sort of thing (instant evil at the end of constant goodness) just does not happen. On the stage, maybe, but not in actual life. There we die as we have lived. The tree that has been tilting toward the south these seventy years does not do a last-minute loop-the-loop and fall north.

True, in any turbulent hour the wind may swing around from southwest to northeast and remain in that quarter for a spell. Any man can be fiercely stirred by some passion and commit a grave sin. But if he is basically sincere, remorse takes over. Like the motorist who has taken a wrong turn, he can't wait to get back on the right road.

The man who is sincere is safe. The phony who tries to serve two masters is in trouble. His soul easily becomes a ghost town. From such a tragedy may the Holy Ghost deliver us!

God Is My Guest

With the feast of Saint Patrick whistling a merry tune just around the bend of the month, there came the memory of this old Irish mother and her tall youngest son who wore his mass of curly black hair like a happy crown. They lived on some little island off the west coast called Innis-something-or-other and sounding like rain on the roof. That particular night she sat knitting in the low room with the firelight dancing against the line of delftware on the shelf, but there was a great worry stirring inside her like a bird that would not be still.

After a while she sighed, then shuffled across the room, and covered the crimson embers with a layer of gray ashes, and felt as if she were burying her own heart. In the morning, when the fire blazed bright again, she knew that he, her youngest, would be going. Now she could hear the sea crooning softly at the foot of the little hill, and it looked lovely out there, wearing the moonlight like a silver scarf. Ah, the sea was a beautiful but seductive woman, and in the morning it would take her boy away. He was going off to make his way in the world.

"I have to, Mom," he had said. "Only the apron strings of God are long enough for me now. The world is like a wide open door coaxing a man to come on."

And that was what she feared, not the sea (though she had seen more than one man brought back wrapped in a sodden and dripping sail) but the world. So in the morning she kissed him sadly, and blessed him with the holy water, and said, "Son of God, go with my son!"

It seems a grand wish, against the background of thatched roof and turf fire and the slight green hill running down to the cove of lapping blue water. We in the big city with the buses and traffic lights and neon signs and hurrying people say simply, "Good-bye." But when you break that phrase down, does it not mean just as much? Does it not really mean, "God be with you"?

But, better still, it does not have to be a mere wish. It can be a glowing, glorious, radiant fact. And that is the whole scope of this little piece: to remind ourselves that if we are in the state of grace, if we are free from serious sin, then our soul is the house of God! God is with us. He dwells within us.

How rarely we remember this consoling and glittering truth! But when we do, it is almost as if we stood on the bank of a great blue lagoon, and gazed into it and saw flashing there the tropical beauties of the deep — wonders we had never dreamed were there. But they are, whether we remember or not.

Consider it again: If your conscience is clean of grave sin, then God Himself with His love is within you. When the special flag flies from the bridge of the aircraft carrier, that means that the admiral is aboard. And if the flag of a clear conscience flies from your soul, this means that God by His grace is really dwelling in your heart.

"Know you not," asks Saint Paul, "that you are the temple of the Holy Spirit?" And Saint John quotes Christ, "If any man love me, I and the Father *will make our abode with him.*"

This then is not painted poetry but solid theological truth — that as long as I am without serious sin, then God is within me, closer to me than the pilot is to the plane or the blossom to the bush. Then the words of the song really become true, "I'll never walk alone!" — because God is always with me.

On Ash Wednesday we have the black smudge of penance on our forehead. On Palm Sunday we hold a sheaf of palm, a memory of Christ, in our hand. Perhaps everyday we wear a tiny religious medal around our neck. Saint Francis Xavier used to keep a copy of his Jesuit vows in a small bag hung over his heart. But these are only outward symbols. How insignificant each of them is, compared to the radiant golden presence of God really within us!

And if God through His grace is really within us, if we actually share in the life of God (and again may I emphasize this is not rose-tinted rhetoric but plain black-and-white doctrine), then religion should never be for any of us a merely negative thing, or a weary obligation, or a stern and depressing routine. Not if we remember that the presence of God burns within us like a flame in a lamp to brighten our everyday life!

In the first place we shall not be looking back in discouraged gloom at past sins, even though they strew the road behind us. The point is they are behind us, and our faces are pointed resolutely forward. Secondly, we shall be kinder to our fellow-man, because if God is within us by His grace, we must always ask ourselves: What would *Christ* do now? And He will remind us that when He walked the earth He had as much time for the loathsome lepers as for the learned lawyers.

Above all we won't be hypocrites going through the hollow motions of religion. I remember once reading about a lady who was drawn toward the Catholic Church but stayed out of it for a long time because of one tiny noise. That particular day she went to lunch with a Catholic girl friend. On the table was a quarter, left there as a tip. The Catholic friend opened her pocketbook and slyly swept the coin in. It clinked against some crystal rosary beads. The other lady said nothing, but she forgot about joining the Church for years.

If you think of the presence of God within you, you don't act like that.

If God is within you, would you not think twice of sinning against Him? Would it not be like playing the informer, the traitor, turning over someone who had taken refuge with you? Especially when you realize what our blessed Lord suffered in order to gain, not man's salvation (one breath would have done that), but man's love.

"What must I do," we can imagine Him asking, "to win man's love? Leave the jeweled and golden glory of Paradise for the rough boards and scraggy straw of a cold cave? I'll do it! Leave the glittering ranks of cherubim and seraphim for the company of dull and earthy peasant shepherds? It shall be done! I'll put down the sizzling white whip of the lightning and even bare my back to the scarlet scourges. I'll put off my dazzling crown of deity for a twisted wreath of thorns, exchange bliss for agony, and give up perfect life for cold, still death. To gain man's love I will do it!"

This is the all-loving, all-generous God who is within us. As much as He was within Mary on the road to Bethlehem, He is within us (if we are free from serious sin) on our rugged road of life. So, let us walk it, happy in that conviction, and determined to be better, kinder, purer; not I, but we! Not me and my shadow, but I and my God!

Virtue Is Not Dull

Did you know that Raphael, surely one of the world's most gifted painters, died at the unlikely age of thirty-seven? I can imagine the cowled monk delivering the eulogy. Probably he held up the artist's untimely end like a holy candle, to illuminate the uncertainty of all human life. Who would have thought that Death would have gently drawn the still-moist brush from those talented fingers, fingers that still glowed with the pink of health and pulsed with the energy of young manhood?

But the funeral procession was more eloquent than the orator, no matter what he said. Behind the casket they carried the canvas that Raphael had been working on when he died, the now world-famous "Transfiguration." Nothing moved the crowds along the line of march like that unfinished masterpiece. How can you portray life's uncertainty more vividly than that?

In Raphael's day it was the custom for a young painter to find a patron who would subsidize his early efforts. This meant flattering the powerful, cultivating the rich, genuflecting before the already famous. In the process it was easy to forget God.

Raphael was more fortunate than most. His genius was early recognized and richly supported. But similar dangers lie around us. We are likely to be so concerned with the many cares of life that we lose sight of the Lord. We have to make a living, but we cannot afford to forget the transcending purpose of life.

When death comes to us, early or late, God will not look into our wallet to see how much we have, or at our diplomas to see how much we know, or at our family tree to examine how distinguished our ancestors. He will look at our soul. Are we His friend or enemy?

From the viewpoint of eternity, in the case of Raphael or any one of us, it does not matter so much how long we live as how we live. But how we live, the whole theme of our life, depends on our code, our convictions. The trouble is, we do not distinguish enough between what is paramount and what is secondary. The world, of course, does not help us to weigh different values, but on the contrary loves to confuse us.

For instance, we moderns are a restless race and any bright weekend sees us whizzing along the highways in pursuit of some distant pleasure. As we speed along, we glance up at the gaudy, flamboyant billboards, those stained-glass windows in the cathedral of commerce. How persuasively they coax us to buy things we really do not need, and which we probably cannot afford, but, oh, we would so like to possess!

Too bad God does not have equal time, or rather equal space. How often have you seen any reminder of God shimmering in neon lights? When was the last time you saw a billboard whose message flamed a reminder of the soul or eternity? If there were many such, it might induce us to go apart to think, just as our Lord went up into the mountain, to be alone. Even sinners, finding themselves alone, have been moved to solemn thinking, as if solitude glared like a huge white spotlight on their conscience.

There was, by way of example, Oscar Wilde, the sophisticated British wit who tossed off flashing epigrams the way a Roman candle spouts gobs of fire. London society crowded around his flowered lapel like peasants around the village well, eager to carry home his latest shining sally. Then came the ghastly revelation. This nimble-tongued intellectual, this elegant dandy, turned out to be a degenerate, and was tossed into prison.

When the iron gates of Reading Gaol clanged shut behind him, practically all his friends proceeded to forget him. Warm admirers suddenly grew cold, and let their former idol rot in loneliness. This started Wilde thinking. The famous playwright looked down upon his sin-scabbed soul in revulsion and near-despair. Then he looked up to the Crucified Christ, pleading for divine pity. And then he wrote his agonizing poem "E Tenebris" ("Out of the Darkness"), which is both a groan of horror and a cry of hope. The Man on the Cross, he was sure, would bend down and send him away forgiven.

Wilde confided that had he been able to kneel before Christ in person, he was sure that this would happen. Sometimes we are tempted to lament that we do not live in the time when Jesus Christ walked the earth. Yet sometimes He seems to treat us even better than He did His contemporaries. For instance, there was that time that our Lord returned to His native Nazareth. By this time He had become famous as the Great Teacher, the Wonder-Worker, the very Messiah. But the envious, small-minded small-towners were so jealous of Him whom they had known only as the carpenter's son, that they tried to fling Him off a cliff. The miracle Jesus performed for them was to walk invisibly through their midst, in order to escape, but He never went back to Nazareth again.

He did come back to Oscar Wilde. Two years after his release from prison, banished from his native country, Wilde lay dying in Paris. Now there was no brilliant repartee, no sensual song about the sweetness of sin, but only a gaunt-eyed whisper asking for a priest. His first Communion was also his last. Once more the old text in the Gospel was verified: The Church was indeed a huge net filled with fish both good and bad.

But none of us, with any sense of human weakness, dare look down a sniffing and scandalized nose at Oscar Wilde or at any public sinner. No man carries in his pocket a guarantee of being good even tomorrow, not to speak of the rest of his life. Look at the sorriest drifter that shambles along skid row, a diary of sin written deep across his dissipated face — can we not say that there, but for the grace of God, go I? Sin is temptation plus opportunity. Many have the temptation but lack foolproof opportunity. What keeps them good is not so much virtue as respectability. They fear to be found out.

Secrecy has always been the devil's strongest argument. It is the silver tray on which every effective temptation is presented. That locked door will guard you. This lonely road will hide you. The darkness will conceal you. No one will ever know. Long ago Shakespeare pointed out that lust and light are eternal enemies. In an extended sense, the ordinary public, the people all around, are like God's policeman. Who wants to shame himself before the world?

But how do we counter when the devil guarantees that no one will ever know, and when all the circumstances seem to bear him out? Simply by reminding ourselves that he is a liar, and that one person, besides ourselves, will always know. In fact, Three Persons, the only Being that matters, God.

To repel temptation, we have our choice of two weapons, fear or love. Fear whispers to me that at every moment of life I am standing on the trapdoor of death. I have no idea when it will be sprung, but I do know that if at that moment my face is turned away from God by grave sin, then it is turned away from Him forever, and I drop into an everlasting hell.

Love takes another tack or tactic. It reminds me that Jesus loved me so much that he laid down his life for me. Shall I not show my gratitude by choosing Him over sin and the devil? Or shall I be another Judas and send him to His death again? Somewhere in his writings, Saint Paul sets down serious sin as a renewal of the Crucifixion.

It will not hurt either, if we remind ourselves that the whole moral law was enjoined by God not to shackle us but to help us. It is there for our benefit, our advantage. Dr. Frank Sheed, the man in the street's theologian, and highly honored by Rome, once made some sharp remarks in this area. I forget the precise words, but Dr. Sheed suspected that there are people who are certain that every now and then a bored God strolls over to the penthouse parapet of heaven, gazes frowningly down on the earth, and mutters, "That human race I made seems to be enjoying itself a little too much down there. Now, let me see, what further can I forbid?"

The fact is, of course, that God never did hang the Ten Commandments on us like handcuffs. He planted them inside us, like our heart or our lungs. They are not imposed from without but exist naturally from within. Long before the Ten Commandments were given to Moses on chiseled tablets, they had been engraved by the Creator on the human conscience. Man knew in his heart that it was wrong to speak falsely, to maim or to murder, to steal another man's wallet or his wife.

However, merely to *know* what is wrong is never enough in the face of strong and vivid temptation. Some of the most brilliant of men have ended up in the moral junkyard. A man's free will can dispose of his conscience like a drugged watchdog while his passions burglarize the house of his soul. At that moment, when temptation is so alluring, and the nondiscovery so reassuring, and any penalty so remote, then only one thought may give us pause: the grim realization that what we do at that moment could decide where we shall spend eternity.

We call it sin. Better if we thought of it as grinding the law of the all-great God beneath our heel, or as flinging the precious blood of Christ back into His face. And this in exchange for what? For a lifetime of luxury, for some high office? More often for something that is gone like the striking of a clock. There are no clocks in eternity.

Even if our dead hands could hold pleasure and power and fame and wealth, what are they all but colored pebbles compared to what Jesus calls the pearl of great price, the saving of our souls, happiness forever? If we fight the good fight and live valiantly for God now, we need not fear about the future, that future that never ends. All He asks is our good will. He will supply the grace.

PART **5**

loaves and fishes

"With This Ring . . ."

When a priest announces his homily theme as matrimony, there will always be a few in his audience whose eyes will harden and whose lips will tighten and whose minds will sourly think, "By what authority does a celibate clergyman lecture us married folk on wedded life? How does a mere spectator in the grandstand dare to ladle out advice to the 'pros' on the field?"

This would be a valid objection if all knowledge bubbled up only from the font of experience. But if this were true, then a lady whose eyes were being slowly clouded by the dim curtain of a cataract, would insist that her surgeon should have had cataracts. Most of us would gladly settle for a man who had twenty-twenty vision. You do not have to have had twins to be a top-flight obstetrician.

Though a priest does not have any personal experience with marriage, in the course of his priesthood he has had contact with many marriages. He has seen them leave the wedding altar like so many little white yachts on a blue sea of happiness. And he has seen too many of them grind to pieces on unsuspected reefs and rocks and wash up as so much driftwood on the rectory shore.

So the priest preaches on marriage, not arrogantly but diffidently, with the basic humility of melancholy hindsight. Besides, since matrimony is a sacrament, is not a priest not only allowed but even obliged to preach on this sacrament?

At any rate, most of the points that a priest would stress for a harmonious marriage would be equally valid for all human beings who are thrown together, whether in offices or colleges or hospitals or clubs. To understand, or to overlook: That attitude will solve so many problems, in or out of marriage.

When people marry very young, there is always the danger that there is too much emphasis on the physical. Such a marriage may quiver on the thin stalk of temporary infatuation rather than be deeply rooted in genuine and lasting love. The boy is swept off his feet by a dimpled face and a fetching figure. The girl is fascinated by shoulders broad as a billboard and a grin like a piano keyboard. He thinks she is luscious. She thinks he is cute. Each of them is infatuated.

In the original Latin, "infatuated" implies the love of a fool. And the fuel in the love of a fool is usually passion, and passion is basically selfish. Passion does not outwardly say so, but inwardly it thinks: What is in it for me? What do I get out of it? Genuine love, on the other hand, asks not what can I get, but what can I give? What can I do to make my loved one happy?

There is more genuine love in the offhand suggestion of a gray-haired wife, thirty years married, to her husband on a slushy February day, "Darling, it is still sloppy out there; you ought to wear your rubbers" — there is more basic love in that, than in the finespun, taffy-sweet line of a modern romantic Romeo. She is not thinking of herself. All her concern is for her loved one.

The mother of a famous English novelist was an enchanting beauty, born to considerable wealth, radiating a sparkling personality, and quite the toast of contemporary London. Her husband, on the other hand, was dangerously close to being stupid and just this side of being ugly. Meanwhile a half-dozen English lords ogled her behind their eager monocles. Any one of them would have been glad to lay his coronet at her dainty feet. Why, her sophisticated circle of friends wondered, did she stay married to this dull, colorless, awkward man? For that she had one pat

119

answer: "He has one tremendous quality. He never hurts my feelings."

Does this sound like *Reader's Digest* religion, or the gospel according to Emily Post? Actually it is scooped right out of Scripture. It is the golden rule of the New Testament: "Do unto others. . . ." And it is more than possible that if some unhappy couples, now living lives of quiet desperation, or sullen frustration, or even dagger-point confrontation, would try to sheathe their hostilities with velvet consideration, then some strange and wonderful things might happen!

Suppose the wife initiates the change. The husband, expecting the usual blast of bitterness, suddenly finds himself swamped with sweetness. What is his reaction? Suspicion, of course. Out of the corner of a wary eye he wonders, "What gives? What is behind all this?"

But if it goes on and on, and every time he expects vinegar he finds he gets whipped cream, he will soon get to love it, and eventually he will love again the source whence it comes. And in this game of love, where hearts are trumps, will he not (even out of mere shame) ultimately follow suit?

It comes down to the ancient and sage counsel of being willing to walk a mile in the other person's moccasins. The husband comes home after a hard day (if you believe him, it is always a hard day) and expects to find his wife neatly groomed, pleasantly smiling, alert, genial, eager to greet him, and the children lined up in a happy little squad ready to intone a reverent chorus of *Hail to the Chief!*

But does he ever stop to think that perhaps his wife has had a hectic day too, between the cooking and the cleaning, the chores and the children — just the children for that matter? Do you recall that yarn about the mother who, on a wintry Sunday morning, as they were about to leave the church, quietly thrust into her husband's hands three small snowsuits, three caps, six assorted mittens, and then started for the door? "What's this?" he

asked. "Oh," she replied, "I thought this morning we'd switch. You dress them and I'll sit in the car and honk the horn."

This is no alibi, of course, for the housewife whose messy and greasy breakfast dishes still repose in the sink under the red rays of a setting sun, the wife who almost always sits down to the evening meal with her hair looking like a feather-duster in a hurricane, the wife whose coat of arms could well be the dial of a clock reading half-past five, surmounting crossed can openers. When you add to all this, slatternly dressing, sloppy housekeeping, a temper like an active volcano and a tongue like an acetylene torch, then you can understand, if not condone, the delaying tactic of a husband who drops into a tavern on his way home, just to fortify himself against what he has to face.

There was one such husband who left one such wife and was hauled before a judge and charged with desertion. "Your Honor," the man said, "if you knew this woman the way I know her, you'd realize that I'm not a deserter. I'm a refugee!"

No question, though, that so often all this can be balanced by looking at the husband's side of the ledger. There is a type of husband who never takes his wife out for recreation, feeling that she should be content to sit at home and admire her wedding ring, and be happy that she has one! Or the husband who, as time writes its diary in the lines on his wife's face, and the bearing and rearing of children blunt her figure, lets his eyes roam to younger and lusher pastures. Then there is the husband who cannot keep the wolf from the door because he pours so much of the family's groceries into the feed bags of horses at racetrack windows. Or the husband who never really sees his responsibilities because he is constantly looking at life through the blurred bottom of a tilted liquor glass.

With a couple married only a short time, the problem can be readjusting to disillusionment. After the novelty of possession and the excitement of passion have died away, like the overture before the play, the curtain goes up on the drama of life as it

121

is really lived: life with its daily routine, its weekly problems, its monthly bills, its constant procession of minor crises. And here are two young people confronted with this, who have never before lived under the same roof. Now in so many ways they discover that the varnish of courtship days quickly peels away, leaving the rough reality beneath. Dispositions rasp and temperaments clash in situations they did not dream.

This is precisely why marriage is bound by a holy vow. This is why marriage is unlike any other contract in the world. It is not like a bill of sale for a car. It is not like a deed for a piece of property. It is not like a promissory note from a bank. This is a contract involving two human beings, two persons, two essentially different individuals. And that is why God elevated matrimony to the eminence of a sacrament. That is why on the very site of the marriage feast of Cana there stands today a small church over whose entrance streams the carved inscription, "What God hath joined, let no man put asunder."

But, if no man may put asunder, sometimes it seems that only God can keep it together. In almost every marriage there may come some desperate hours when either the pilot or the copilot feels like jumping out, pulling the rip cord and hoping for the best. That is the time to remember what we priests forget to emphasize: the spiritual capital of sanctifying grace.

Nearly fifty years ago a bishop laid his hands on my head, placed in my hands a chalice, and ordained me a young priest. Was I then on my own? Was I supposed from that day on to climb the steep path of the priesthood with no supporting staff? By no means! With that sacrament of ordination I received, as it were, a spiritual bankbook, a savings account of graces to draw from. Thereafter, as long as I lived, in any crisis in my priestly life, in any dark hour, angry hour, frustrated hour, tempted hour, I had only to present my credentials and say, "Lord, You gave me the sacrament. Now give me the grace!" And He has, He must, He will!

Do you mean to tell me that the golden ring of matrimony is less a sacrament than the golden chalice of ordination? It is not! So in any thorny hour, any clouded hour of your marriage, you can do the same. You can say, "Lord, You gave me the sacrament. Now give me the grace, the special help I need here and now!"

Go through our Lady. Ask through her. If at the wedding feast of Cana, Mary obtained a miracle (even an unscheduled miracle: "My hour is not yet come") just to keep a wedding breakfast from falling apart, she can obtain for you, if necessary, even a miracle to hold your marriage together. But usually a miracle is not needed: just a little more consideration, a little more thoughtfulness for the other party, a little more truly unselfish love!

Fathers Without Children

While it is true that in Church matters I am usually rated by my friends (sometimes I suspect by both of them) as being quite conservative, I am not yet so attached to the old that I look with suspicion even upon the new moon. After all, there are conservatives and conservatives, just as there are pirates and pirates. Not too long ago at a banquet I caught sight of a rather prominent layman from another state. I knew he was conservative enough to drive a total of some sixty miles each Sunday to attend a Latin Mass in a monastery chapel. I hasten to add that this liturgy is not the abolished Tridentine but the approved modern version.

I thought he would not remember me, so I held out my hand and said, "Father Manton." He smiled wickedly and said, "And how is Mrs. Manton?" — implying that like some of the New Breed I had perhaps decided to do a little breeding. I replied with perhaps the glint of an icicle in my own smile that I trusted that Mrs. Manton, my good mother, was at that mo-

123

ment high in heaven, and hoped that one day he might even come within telescope distance of her.

He was joking, of course, but subsequent conversation showed that he by no means took the matter of priestly celibacy lightly. Neither do the vast majority of the Catholic laity whom I happen to encounter, but whom the pollsters seem to miss. These people are by no means flippant about celibacy, nor indifferent to the issue, but strongly in favor of unwived priests. In the pages of magazines or on the talk shows of television you may meet recently married priests who cry down celibacy, but the average Catholic may meanwhile be wondering if such a cleric does not have an ax to grind, or a conscience to quiet, or perhaps a book to sell.

If you could line up all the people and priests who are in favor of a celibate clergy, I doubt that they would be outnumbered or outvoted by the aggressive opposition. For a while they are merely being outshouted.

The stand of the official Church is all for celibacy. Canon law (still in force) calls for celibacy. The Second Vatican Council supported celibacy. The first international synod of bishops endorsed celibacy. The encyclical of Paul VI stood behind celibacy. When you have canon law, council, synod and the Sovereign Pontiff speaking the same words, does this not reflect the attitude and the spirit of the Church?

Against all this, what is the thrust of the opposition? It is true that in the wake of Vatican II there was an earthquake of defections. But since then the tremors have been less and less. Does anyone hear a piercing cry for relief from the overwhelming vast majority of priests, the ones that stayed, not the faithful departed? Is there a surging roar rising from the Catholic laity, demanding a married clergy?

One string on the anti-celibacy guitar that has been strummed till it must be on the point of snapping, is the strong emphasis placed on the point that celibacy is not essential to the

priesthood. If ever a straw man has been carefully fashioned and triumphantly bayoneted, this is it. Don't they remember that even the Council of Trent (which modern theology smilingly regards as paleontology, and which enjoined celibacy) was also careful to underline that celibacy was not of the essence of the priesthood? What pope ever claimed it was? How *could it be*, in the light of all those married Apostles? Sterile gloves are not of the essence of the surgeon either, but they do have some significant advantages.

Certainly an unmarried priesthood is not a divine command. But just as certainly the Church has always looked upon celibacy undertaken for the love of God as a higher spiritual state. Surely, celibacy is not of the essence of the priesthood, but just as surely the Church has found that the priesthood is exercised better with celibacy and through celibacy. In the cold white light of experience, celibacy shows up even as more practical. Here, it is not a question of what is more convenient or more comfortable for the individual priest, but of what is better for the Church and the Gospel.

Some might object that a celibate priesthood deprives a man of one of his inalienable rights: the right to marry. Yes, but on the other hand he does not have an inalienable right to become a priest; and if he accepts that vocation, he must accept the conditions that go with it. He is not trussed up and carried off to the priesthood. He enters willingly, after years of reflection and preparation. The priesthood did not join him. He joined the priesthood, and its obligations.

Theology teaches that a vocation is a two-way street: the desire to become a priest on the part of the candidate, and the acceptance of the candidate by the Church. The aspirant carefully reads the contract and solemnly signs his name — in essence it amounts to that. Of course, if the stipulations involved anything sinful, it would be a different matter and the contract automatically invalid. But it doesn't.

Or it may be alleged that celibacy, considering human nature, is not natural. For that matter, considering human nature and original sin and the weakening of the will and the revolt of the passions, fidelity to one woman is not "natural." Take away supernatural help and it is "natural" for the eyes of a married man to stray to lusher pastures and younger women. So we have infidelities and adulteries, mistresses and paramours.

Therefore, should we abolish marriage? Should it be replaced with polygamy or promiscuity? For a man to keep his marriage vow there must be self-discipline and self-control and absolute dedication to the keeping of his solemn word. But this is precisely what is required of the celibate too. More than one priest who is married has discovered that the very virtues he has to practice now in matrimony are exactly the ones that he should have practiced when he was a celibate priest.

What the Church enjoins in celibacy is not the impossible, but the difficult. It is impossible to live without eating and drinking and breathing, but it is not impossible to live without sex. From the sacrament of holy orders will come, if the priest earnestly asks it, the sturdy staff to help him climb the steep hill.

But let us be fair. Nobody in the other camp is insisting on obligatory celibacy. What they graciously offer is optional celibacy. Let each seminarian and each priest opt for his choice. This is all the more magnanimous when you reflect that all the surveys (bow your head at that word) indicate that at this point in time the grand majority of priests would not marry even if the golden chains were stricken from their sacerdotal limbs.

But, note carefully, that is *now*. This is against a background of celibacy going back for centuries. However, suppose that next week celibacy were repealed, like Prohibition. During the next twenty years there would evolve, naturally, a climate for marriage. What would a similar survey reveal in the year 2000?

Optional celibacy is a mirage. Or it is the vestibule to a nonexistent, extinct celibacy. The Presbyterians have optional celibacy; the Episcopalians have optional celibacy; the Methodists have optional celibacy. They all have optional celibacy — but how many celibates?

Others suggest: Why not permit diocesan priests to marry and let the order priests stay celibate? But are not the reasons for celibacy the same for all priests? Optional celibacy has a sweetly reasonable sound, and making a distinction between the secular and religious priesthood may appear eminently logical; but when the Church riffles through the grim pages of its old, tattered diary, it shows optional celibacy just will not work.

The Church remembers the Reformation, when morals were at their scummiest low tide, when clerical concubinage was rampant and when chastity was for the saints. During that age the Church, the ship of Peter, certainly should have gone gurgling down in a sea of dirty water, except for one thing: Christ was aboard. Those were the days when, under the encouragement of the "reformers" (who should have reformed the morals of the churchmen instead of the doctrines of the Church), the diocesan priests entered wedlock on all sides. But how swiftly the monks poured out of the monasteries to follow them! Soon there were ten thousand married ex-priests, diocesan and monastic.

It is a curious little footnote of those times that Luther, who opened the doors for the rush, himself neatly stepped aside, not marrying for five years after he had left the Church. He had been an Augustinian monk and eventually married a former nun. When he did marry, he implied it was not to allay concupiscence but to please his father and to spite the devil and the Pope. The reaction of neither is on record.

Some scholars think that celibacy had its origin in the concept of ritual purity. The rituals of ancient civilizations believed there should be no conjugal relations before the offering of sacrifice or the solemn act of worship. Some of this went over into the Old Testament and eventually seeped into Christianity.

Around the fifth century, when Mass began to be celebrated each day, there seemed to be only one way of abstaining from conjugal privileges before offering the holy sacrifice of the Mass, and that was to be without a wife. So celibacy sprang from the intimate association of the priesthood with the Eucharist.

The celibate priest does not deny the beauty of married love. He recognizes it and reluctantly gives it up for a higher love, the undivided love of God. Does anyone think that a man cannot serve his fellowmen unless he also loves one particular woman?

Most priests who give up the priesthood and get married (at least the ones I have encountered) will tell you that they did not take off the cassock in order to get married, or, as we used to say, tripped over a hairpin. I think this is true. Some believed they got a raw deal from a pastor or bishop; some were frustrated because they could not get the green light for a cherished pastoral undertaking; some were discontented about assignments or disappointed about advancement. The soft shoulder did not force them off the road, but it was there for them to weep on when they went off. Sensuality or sex did not load the gun. It only pulled the trigger.

As I recall, the Pope requested that there be no discussion of celibacy at Vatican II, but the document approved by the bishops said this: "Continence was recommended by Christ the Lord. . . . [Celibate priests] more easily hold fast to Him with [a free and] undivided heart. They [can] more freely devote themselves to Him and through Him to the service of God and men" (*The Documents of Vatican II*, "Decree on the Ministry and Life of Priests"). With a married priesthood would the Gospel be better preached and the Church better off? With a married priesthood would a parish be better run, the sick better cared for, the school better administered? Would a married priesthood present a more radiant image of Christ and religion?

There are, to be sure, outside the Roman rite (like the

Byzantine) Catholic priests in our day who are married. But note that these rites choose for their bishops only priests who are celibate or at least widowers.

The truth is that in sponsoring celibacy the Church is motivated by a selfishness as low as the crawling ocean floor, and yet also by a spiritual idealism as high as a snow-crowned Alp. Selfishly (or perhaps practically is the better word) the Church wants an unmarried clergy because it is easier to support one man than a whole family, because it is easier to transfer one man than a whole household, because it is easier to assign one man without a family to a dangerous spot like a military chaplaincy or a remote one like a foreign mission. Here the Church thinks like Standard Oil or IBM.

At the other end of the scale, where the notes climb high and spiritual, the Church believes that its priests should demonstrate that they believe what they preach; and in this respect you cannot give better testimony to your belief in the supernatural than by giving up the natural. The lonely bed is a proof that the priest is not playing games.

It is often brought up that a married priest would make a better marriage counselor. When I mentioned this once to a married minister, he smiled wryly, saying, "Father, when a couple come to you with their problem, you probably have to suggest some compromises, which neither is willing to make, and so they tell you, 'You wouldn't understand, Father. You're not married.' A similar pair comes to me, and I give them the same advice. But they shake their heads and say, 'You wouldn't understand, Reverend. Your marriage is happy.' "

It follows with Thomistic logic that what the Catholic Church needs in the way of marriage counselors is about ten thousand unhappily married priests.

All this is not to say that celibacy will be with us forever. We have seen more changes in Church ritual and practices and procedure (not doctrines, though) in the last dozen years than have happened in the previous half-dozen centuries. It is altogether possible, therefore, that the Church may make a few relaxing adjustments in the knot of celibacy. Perhaps the clergy may be permitted to marry in certain countries where priests are scarce, and distances vast, and the man in a cassock leads a remote, solitary life, rarely even seeing another priest.

There is less likelihood that an early change will happen in the United States. The reasons that brought celibacy into being in the first place are still strongly valid here. To sum up: From the merely practical point of view, a priest who is without wife and family can be supported more cheaply, can give more time to the service of God and people, can take more risks with less worry, and can be more easily uprooted and reassigned as the needs of his diocese or his order dictate.

From the spiritual angle, celibacy for the priest is a closer following of Christ, his model. For the people it is a proof that he believes so firmly in the supernatural that he is willing to sacrifice the natural. Thus a love which is nobler than the sensual can flow out into all that broader family that universally salutes the celibate priest as "Father."

parish, school, world

Fireside of the Soul

Among the vast, elegant and even awesome churches on this continent, I think that most observers would rank high the Basilica of St. Anne de Beaupre, some twenty miles north of Quebec. Yet the original church there was a tiny chapel of rough logs. Stand today in the nearby mossy old cemetery, among the time-tilted crosses and the slanting gray slabs of the headstones, and you are standing among French missionaries and Indian converts who have been lying there for three hundred years.

Riffle through the old baptismal register in the rectory and you can read neatly penned entries in ink that has rusted with the centuries, testifying to babies and godparents who flourished circa 1660. Then if you glance out the window toward the modern highway approaching the towered basilica, you may smilingly ponder how Abbé Morel, the first pastor, would have blinked his dark French eyes in amazement if he could see this line of shining cars with license plates from South Carolina to South Dakota, dropping in to visit the modern Shrine of St. Anne. In the midst of his great green wilderness has gone up a tiny granite city of God: monastery and seminary and convent and hospital. But most imposing and impressive of all, the basilica.

From log chapel to frame church to stone edifice to massive

basilica — is not this also the history of the Church itself? Has not the Church gone from Bethlehem's stable to the catacombs to parish churches to majestic cathedrals? The original log chapel at Beaupre was built by Breton sailors who had vowed that if they survived that furious and historic storm they would erect a shrine to their patroness, La Bonne Ste. Anne, on the very spot they landed. This miraculous survival at sea was a gloriously fitting backdrop for the building of a church, because ever since our Savior stepped into the bark of Peter on the lake of Galilee, spiritual men have always thought of a church in terms of a ship.

Like a ship, a church always has a name. Like a ship, a church generally has a bell. Like a ship, a church often has a tapering spire tipped with a cross that soars up like a mainmast. And the general interior of the church is called the nave, which is the Latin word for ship, as witness *naval* battle.

Show me a Catholic church and I will show you a fishing ship whose nets are the finely woven mesh of the confessional screens where souls are caught for God. Show me a Catholic church and I will show you a cargo ship whose prayers and hymns and indulgences and resolutions are stored away for export to heaven. Show me a Catholic church and I will show you a battleship, from whose pulpit thunder the guns of God, as sin is bombarded, pagan principles blasted and virtue defended. Show me a Catholic church and I will show you a passenger ship whereby the people of God are carried across the wild waters of this hostile world to the safe haven and happy heaven of the eternal shore.

But if a church is a passenger ship, there is one shattering difference: There are no doors that divide the wealthy and the middle class and the poor, no "First Class" or "Cabin Class" or the old scornful "Steerage." The church is a twentieth-century Bethlehem where the poor and the unschooled kneel in the pews with the rich and the educated, as the shepherds knelt next to the Wise Men in the Christmas stable. The church is a modern Calvary where there stand beneath the cross not only saints like John the Apostle and Mary the stainless Virgin Mother, but also sinners like the stained Mary Magdalene. The church is a contemporary Nazareth, a fireside of the soul, where one can come in out of the cold world for a spell and spiritually warm his hands and say a friendly word to the Holy Family — Jesus, Mary and Joseph.

A church is a building standing among other buildings, but it is like none of them. No brazen, garish neon sign dances before it, proclaiming, "Look at me, here I am!" It has only the tiny red flame of the tabernacle light, often fluttering in half darkness. No belching chimney twists its black banner of smoke above the church. Only now and then a thin blue swirl of incense curls fragrantly before the altar. No throbbing machinery vibrates the walls. On the contrary the usual atmosphere is a sacred quiet.

The church does not manufacture any product. If it were a linoleum factory you could ask just how many yards or even miles of linoleum it turned out during a year. But there are no loading platforms in the rear where linoleum or shoes or shirts are packaged in huge cartons and sent off. What a church produces cannot be packed in boxes or poured into barrels. How do you measure or package peace of heart, courage restored, forgiveness sought and received?

A church's output is something more precious than material commodities. Its product is not goods but *good*. Its product is faith and hope and love of fellowman, and patience in little trials, and resignation under big crosses. Here a man can find clear-eyed resolution and unflinching dedication to the worthwhile things of life.

Only God knows how many a worried mother has stolen into the almost empty church, and in that serene climate of prayer has slipped off the sack of care that bent her down, and later walked out with a high and shining spirit. Only heaven is aware how many people who were sick unto spiritual death with sins that blotched their souls like smallpox felt the healing finger of God in the church's confessional.

Sophisticates may mock the old woman who shuffles into a church bench, sits down and rattles her beads and prays in a sibilant whisper. They may smile patronizingly at the young girl who goes clicking down the aisle on her spike heels and lights a votive light to illumine the way on the treacherous path of love. They may shrug at the sight of a man in working clothes slipping in for a visit on his way home from the job, a mechanic perhaps laying his family problems before the Carpenter. But the fact is that these people are humbly and lovingly lifting their eyes to their Father who is in heaven, and He blesses them, steadies them, guides them, reassures them.

The days in our lives that most stand out, like steeples over rooftops, have been days that brought us to church: the day when the baptismal water streamed across our pink baby brow, the day when we knelt trembling in the dark confessional box for the first time and timorously whispered that we had "distobeyed" and were (ironically) sorry for all the sins "of our past life," the day when we knelt with our chin just reaching the altar rail and received our first Holy Communion. Red-and-green Christmases, golden Easters, and perhaps a gloriously happy white wedding, or possibly a heartbreaking black funeral — so many important pages in our lives have rising behind them the solemn background of an altar and a church!

As you ride through a Catholic region, whether Quebec or Bavaria or Ireland, you realize that it is no accident that the church is the center point of the community, the hub of the wheel. For the church is not just so much wood and stone or steel and concrete — it is a sacred thing, a place apart, a symbol of the highest and best in the human spirit. Its stained-glass windows are more than rainbows locked in frames; they are the blazing symbols of the truths these people live by, like a perpetual sunset casting its colors on the pictures in an old family Bible.

The very bell is part of the parish, hanging high and ringing clear, sometimes tumbling wildly in the drenching storm, sometimes clanging sharply through the whirling snow — calling, coaxing, scolding, pleading, commanding, jigging for joy (it seems) on Christmas Eve and tolling like the slow beat of a heavy heart when someone's loved one is sadly rolled down the aisle under the flickering yellow candles out toward the silent waiting hearse.

To the sincere Catholic no building stands for more than his church, whether that church be a squat square of painted boards or a granite temple with twin spires soaring toward the skies. Culture gives us the opera house and the art museum; politics gives us the state capitol and the town hall; industry gives us the factory; travel gives us the hotel; but religion gives us the church. It is man standing on tiptoe and straining upward with his fingertips to touch God. It is the creature acknowledging his Creator, and not merely acknowledging but also adoring, appeasing, beseeching. It is the material making contact with the spiritual. Though the church be only so much wood or stone and though these will inevitably crumble, the prayers said under its roof, the resolutions made under its influence, the ten thousand good deeds done under its inspiration — all these will roll like waves to the distant and everlasting shores of eternity.

Lower Education

There is a special kind of silence that goes with the Egyptian wing of an art museum, a kind of ancient, musty vacuum. There is a type of silence, too, that goes with the reading room of a stuffy leather-chaired club, where *a*'s are broader and views narrower, and where the rustling of a turned newspaper page seems like a raucous intrusion. But the silence that drops down like a leaden lid on a schoolyard in summer has a blank stillness all its own. You feel you are looking at a great, empty, abandoned nest.

The wriggling and the romping, the running and the jumping, the screams and the squeals, the games and the laughter have suddenly grown still, and it is hard to get used to it. In the school itself the long green shades are drawn all the way, as though it were a wake and the spirit of childhood had died. Perhaps in this classroom or that the windows are open and the swish of the paintbrush is soft on the air.

But where, meanwhile, are the nuns? Taking a summer course in something or other. Trudging the endless academic treadmill to some degree. When it is ninety degrees outside, the nuns are inside working on another. Or they may be teaching in summer school. Or making their annual spiritual retreat. At best there comes to their tight schedule the brief breath of a week or two without assignment when they can throw their weary brain into neutral and gratefully coast. At least the older nuns remember it so!

But it is the children who have emptied the school yard. In this blessed interval what is happening to them? They are eating like steam shovels, sleeping like tombstones, playing like perpetual motion machines, and growing like beanstalks. But one thing about them is not growing. It is, if anything, losing. In the shallow pond of their little brain the hot summer sun seems to dry up almost everything that was patiently poured into it during the past nine months. When school reopens in the fall and the teacher holds the first review, she will marvel that they were able to forget so much in so short a time. Sister Listerina in the seventh grade will wonder if her pupils ever learned anything in the sixth. Meanwhile Sister Oleomargarina in the eighth grade is thinking pretty much along the same lines about Sister Listerina's exports from the seventh.

How shallow our learning process can be! School is out and in the average home any class books or homework books are tossed into the limbo of some forgotten closet till after Labor Day. All this time no school bell rings, no teacher makes an assignment, no page is turned, no ballpoint touches paper, because no parent is interested.

Perhaps I had better take that back and make a distinction. In homes where the father is a doctor or a lawyer or any sort of professional man, or in a home where the mother is a college graduate, or in a home where the children are at the top of their classes, in other words in homes where they need it least — this is precisely where the books do occasionally come out and there are casual, informal sessions of review. It is tragic but it is true that just as you can say, "The poorer the neighborhood, the more saloons," so also the poorer the neighborhood the more indifference to the children's schoolwork. (A poor Jewish neighborhood would be an exception to both of these rules, and I honor them for it.)

I am not advocating scholastic child slavery in the summer. But if you look at other lands you will find that their vacations are much shorter, their school day longer, their programs harder, and yet the youngsters survive and emerge ahead of ours. In our long vacation would a little home review each week really hurt? Could there not at least be a couple of sessions of spelling and of reading, areas in which the youngsters of today are pathetically weak?

If the child did return to school remembering the capital of Rumania or the boundaries of Russia, it is possible that the geography teacher might collapse over her spinning globe with a heart attack, but at least she would die happy. With just a little interest in the home during the summer, the teacher would not have to face the frustrating job each September of trying to touch the spark of learning to a young mind that is hopelessly sopping wet after being submerged for three months in the waters of complete mental idleness.

Certainly children will not like the idea of a bit of review. Is this a valid reason for rejecting it? What are the first three words a child learns? Possibly *Da-da*, *Ma-ma*, and *No*! And not necessarily in that order.

A child's mind is a curious machine. It learns fast and it forgets fast. The same lad who in June could answer catechism questions (like, what is a sacrament or an indulgence) stumbles over the Hail Mary in September. The explanation hits you like a slap in the face: During July and August he has not been saying the Hail Mary. Let parental supervision doze, and morning prayers yield to the Breakfast of Champions. Night prayers might fare slightly better, but God still must have huge stacks of rain checks for night prayers that were called off.

Another baffling mystery is the disappearance of the long squirming lines of schoolchildren that stretch out from the confessionals during the school year. They will be back, of course, like the swallows at Capistrano, and saying, "My last confession was three months ago." A vacation is good and useful and necessary. For adults a vacation from confession is like a vacation from soap and water. It leaves you grimy in yourself and no sweet influence on others. For children regular confession builds a beneficial habit.

What, after all, is the purpose of the parochial school? Is it just to put into the young brain, like stamps in an album, the dates and the decimals, the capitals and the fractions? Is it not also supposed to provide religious training, motives, ideals and spiritual formation? But neither the church nor the school can do this alone. Neither was ever supposed to. Fundamentally all this is the responsibility of the Catholic home. They are not the church's children nor the school's children but the family's children. Isn't there something wrong when, as soon as vacation comes and the school closes, good practices seem to stop? Is it too much to ask the parents to give the children the same attention in July as they expect the nuns to give them in January?

Many a youngster can maneuver his parents like a yo-yo on

a string. The parents are so fond of him; he is such a clean-cut boy. They are so fond of her; she is such a darling girl. So almost any request is approved. Parents should be kind, but they should not be blind. The bitterest voice a priest ever hears is one that says, "When I was young, my parents let me get away with anything."

Youngsters need guidance most of all during the summer vacation, when the devil's turnstiles click their busiest. A conscientious parent will insist on a program that calls for morning and night prayers regularly, weekday Mass occasionally, Sunday Mass always, and the sacraments frequently. This is not callous tyranny, but farsighted love. And one day when the children reach their maturity, like bonds, the gilt-edged coupons you clip will be gratitude and respect. Gilt, not guilt.

Beyond Education

You don't hear him mentioned often these days, but in the second century he was one of the really radiant lights on the candlestick of the Church. Some perhaps might put him down in his latter years as a flamboyant heretic. At any rate, this man Tertullian maintained among other things that the human soul was naturally Christian.

So bald and bold an assertion might have set some undoubtedly devout men, like Abraham and Moses, to stroking their beards in bewilderment. Perhaps their eyebrows would come down if Tertullian had been content to claim that the human soul was naturally religious.

Through the centuries Everyman, buffeted by daily minor disasters and groping along a road curtained by fog, has looked for a meaning behind the mystery of life. He stumbles along, seeking a purpose and a guide.

However, in his younger days, Everyman does not usually

accept religion gladly. In fact the feisty years of young manhood often tend to reject religion. Almost by nature youth is inclined to rebel against authority, including religious authority. Youth resents this dictatorial delivery of dogmas. It bristles at the high-handed handing down of doctrines without so much as a by-your-leave. "Independent thinking" is the password of the young. They want proof, incontrovertible, steel-plated proof. They want to know the day, the hour, the place, the length, the height, the whole bit.

If you offer as proof the word of God, you may get a smile that is first cousin to a smirk. If you appeal to miracles, the young shoulders will shrug off events that happened so long ago and so far away. (As though, if something really did happen, any passage of time could erode it, or any measure of miles could annihilate it.)

By the same token, youth will accept the Holy Spirit only if you can produce a passport photo and some unsmudged fingerprints. But by that same test there does not exist any such thing as an idea, a memory, a hope, or even a youthful doubt.

For youth there can never be on the map of human knowledge any *Terra Incognita*, any Unknown Territory. Youth has to know everything. It never dawns on youth that if it knew as much as God, it would be God. Only God knows the answers to many questions, the solutions to many problems. Only God has the key to many doors. And the first sure step that adolescence takes into adulthood is to realize that as mere human beings we do not and cannot ever know it all.

With maturity comes a clearer viewpoint. Quietly, subtly, gradually, religion does begin to make some sense. More light pours in through the stained-glass windows. The mature adult notices that as each new generation snaps its fingers at religion and turns on its heel to walk away from the Church, it often marches across the street to the temple of Science. Here the votive lights are Bunsen burners or Etna lab lamps. Here the articles of devotion are not bell, book and candle, but test tube, slide rule and computer.

But now the conviction seeps in. This new world of Science is founded upon order. All these atoms and molecules, these protons and neutrons and electrons, are not assembled in a haphazard grab bag. They do not combine at random; nor do they represent an accident — they form an intricate, interlocking pattern. And behind all this precision ought to be something, or more correctly, Someone. The Engineer behind the engine.

Out there, somewhere, there has to be God. Not conspicuous, not blatant, but there, just as quiet and just as strong as the law of gravitation. It reminds you of the boy and his kite. He was flying it early one summer morning on the lawn before a White Mountain hotel. The mist had come down, and in a little while he stood there, surrounded by a great fog that hung like a gray, dripping sail. A visitor strolled out on the porch and noticed the boy standing there and apparently holding on to a piece of string. "What are you doing?" the man asked. "I'm flying my kite," said the boy. "I don't see any kite," said the man. "Neither do I," said the boy, "but I can feel its pull."

As we mature, more and more we sense the presence of God and feel His pull. And we need Him around us, because Science with all its towering achievements does not give us even a clue to the ultimate meaning of existence. "Why am I here? Where am I headed?" Ask Science these questions and you get only a glazed stare.

Science can provide progress, and progress supplies improvement: improvement in our food and our shelter, our health, our travel, our communication. Science can provide mathematically sliced bread, split-level houses, double-knit fabrics, air-conditioned cars, even miracle drugs. But does not all this merely add up to making man a healthier and more comfortable animal? In the vast libraries of Science, you will not find even one slim volume that assures the well-fed and well-dressed man that his brilliant years are not just a meaningless journey toward a spot where Death stands leaning on a shovel beside a waiting grave.

Master of a thousand islands, Science does not touch the mainland. And that is why through the centuries man has stood on his tiptoes and reached up with his fingertips, straining to touch the supernatural, to find the answer to why he is here, to seek forgiveness for secret guilt, to contact the God who made it all, and who understands it all.

Can this life, the thinking man asks himself, lead to just nothing? He looks around at the skyscrapers and the cathedrals, the plays of Shakespeare, the paintings of Michelangelo, the symphonies of Beethoven, men walking on the moon, the noble hearts he has admired and loved, and he asks himself: Is this the end of it all, to be lowered in the ground as a box lunch for the worms, or to be only so many powdery gray ashes on a king-size ash tray in a crematorium?

But this is only part of the picture. Youth rebels against religion not only on the intellectual level but perhaps even more on the physical plane. Is not youth the time when a man first feels his oats and perhaps has a tendency to sow a few wild ones? But along comes religion, like a frowning schoolteacher with an admonishing finger, screaming a forbidding "No!" Here comes the stern injunctions, the grim prohibitions, the thundering "You shall not's!"

Poor youth! He not only must yield to the Creed what he must believe, but also to the Ten Commandments what he must do, or what is often harder, what he must not do. But youth is supposed to be the days of wine and roses! So why should the wine be soured into vinegar, and the roses sharpened into thorns? Why must he have to bow his intellect to the Creed, and his passions to the commandments of God?

Strangely, though, as adolescence becomes adulthood, as the brash and breezy days of life's springtime become the more serene and sedate autumn, the viewpoint changes. For one thing, the grown man begins to realize that even though each new generation hoots at faith and heckles religion, religion and faith serenely march into the next century.

Perhaps now he is a parent and thinking only in terms of protecting his own daughter. But as he looks back, he recognizes that those restraints imposed by religion were not really the spiteful bars of a jail meant to keep him from happiness, but were rather the guardrails on a bridge, there to protect him from falling to moral ruin.

At last he realizes that religion, precisely because of its restraints, is the main arch in the whole temple of civilization. Religion — with its high ideals, its lofty moral codes, its supernatural truths, its eternal sanctions — provides the sturdy pillars to support right and order and common decency. Parents employ religion in raising their children. The State welcomes religion because it develops a responsible citizenry. Without the moral assistance of religion, there could not be enough policemen to keep the world respectable.

Youth does not want to submit either its proud brain or its eager flesh. But as man grows older, he stirs with a new hunger that goes beyond these. In his deepest soul man yearns to survive. He feels intimations of immortality. He has within himself a strange, restless yearning that the world around him cannot satisfy: not the natural world with its gorgeous sunsets, not the mechanical world with its superb technology, not the social world with its whirl of parties, not the scholarly world with its shelves of books. He is reaching out for something more, and in reaching he finds religion, God, the Church.

Here is an age-old faith to lean on, like a strong staff for the mysterious journey. Here is an expert guide that will infallibly point the way. Here is stately ritual that will lift up one's heart in inspiration, and lay a soothing calm on a disturbed spirit. Here are old familiar hymns that can turn the driest throat into a bell tower chiming with joy and hope. And here are fellow believers kneeling in the neighboring pews, like tiny silver streams that merge into a great, sweeping river of faith.

He looks about him, and the devout statues remind him of the millions who have said their prayers before him. He remembers the long line of crimson martyrs who have given their lives for this Creed. He feels reassured.

It is not easy for young or old to humble the mind and accept the Creed, or to subdue the flesh and conform to the commandments. But when our last day is done, when the hour comes to close shop, and turn the key in the lock, and leave the money in the till, and when it is time to walk the dark road alone, then it will be good to lift one's dimming eyes and see candle and crucifix, holy water and sacred oils, and the priest with the little white host.

Everything grows simple at the end. No sophistication, no pretense, no status. This is it. Tomorrow is eternity. As someone said a long time ago, "The Catholic faith may be a hard religion to live in, but it is certainly a good one to die in."

Knothole Catholics

Whatever it is that separates the men from the boys, it is the Society for the Propagation of the Faith that separates the knothole Catholics from the wide-world, vista-vision Catholics. A knothole Catholic is one who squints one eye through a tiny hole in a fence and can see no farther than his own spiritual backyard, the local parish. What results almost comes down to a Catholic faction as opposed to Catholic Action. The adjective derived from "parish" is "parochial," and one meaning of "parochial" is "narrow-minded." On the other hand, the meaning of "Catholic" is "wide, broad, universal across the world." So declares the dictionary.

Probably the closest most of us come to seeing the Catholic

Church in action in this universal sense is the miniature we may encounter at a mission exhibit. A few years ago, I wandered through a big one at the Boston Garden. (For the uninitiated, Boston Garden is actually a balconied arena. As a garden, it is more famous for gladiators than for gladioli, and in the realm of flowers it really never got farther than cauliflower ears. On this occasion of the mission exhibit, it was like the Christians taking over the Roman Colosseum.)

Anyway, as you strolled around the two hundred exhibition booths, it was like sauntering through the international village of some spiritual Olympics. So many nations were represented on the huge floor that you realized that the Catholic Church actually did arch the world like a rainbow, and like a rainbow glowed with the colors of every race. When it came to priests, I was most fascinated by the men on the African mission who wore long white robes and bright red turbans.

The costumes at the booths gave the scene a United Nations air. You saw the furry Eskimo, the blanketed Navajo, the kimonoed Japanese. There were knives from New Guinea, swords from Thailand, butterfly trays from Brazil. You realized, though, that these were only exotic souvenirs brought back by the missionaries, the Church's own Foreign Legion, now home on a brief furlough, chiefly for the pleasure of us stay-at-homes.

But all the time you knew that what you saw in the cheery and well-lighted mission exhibit was the superficial glamour without the actual hardships. You saw the gay trinkets but not the grim trials. You saw the romance of faraway places but not the monotony of plodding the same routine road between the same villages week after week. You did not feel the bite of vicious flies. You did not have to wince at the crawling insect life. Your stomach did not go queasy from greasy food. Your tongue did not stammer over strange sounds. You did not feel the heartache of leaving home and dear ones, nor the loneliness of landing in an alien place where you were not particularly wanted, bringing a religion that was not welcome, and feeling that in the face of such huge pagan indifference you were like a man with a nail file attacking the Rocky Mountains.

Why, then, go on the foreign missions at all? Because our Commander in Chief, Jesus Christ, gave the order: "Go into the whole world and preach the Gospel to every creature." Obviously not every Christian can leave home and take the faith to far-off lands. For that matter, in an army not every soldier fights. Behind the man with the rifle must stand four or five other men, bringing up ammunition, food, gasoline, clothing, medicine, maps and the like. In much the same way, there must be men and women behind every foreign missionary. *We* must be their backers-up and not be "just the folks back home."

Pope Pius XII said a startling thing about helping the foreign missions. He declared: "As heaven is above earth, giving to the foreign missions is above every other charity." He did not say that other works of charity were not commendable. If you build a hospital or a home for the aged, certainly you give them health or comfort for a few years of their natural life. But if you give to the Propagation of the Faith you are helping souls toward eternal life. In a sense you are giving heaven.

There is another motive for helping the foreign missions. As Americans have we no honor? Have we no memory? Do we not recognize a legitimate spiritual debt? Was there not a time, in fact for centuries, when we were on the receiving end? The Church had its beginning in America because priests from well-established parishes or monasteries in a cultivated Europe came to the American wilderness. The very roots of our religion in the United States were nourished by the blood and bones of these exiles to America. And, not only men but also means came from Europe to found our first parishes. Catholic foreign mission societies on the continent sent steady streams of francs and talers and guilders and pesos to help emigrants establish the faith of their fathers.

Now that the United States is the world's most prosperous nation, should we not pay our religious debt by helping to bring the Church to needy lands like Asia and Africa? Let our exports to such places be not just soft drinks and computers but also Christian learning and culture, not just tools from our factories but the truths of our faith, not just good machines but good men! A priest or Brother or Sister can be America's best representative in the less progressive parts of the world. Gradually the people realize that here is someone who does not come to exploit their market but only to save their souls. Here is one who comes not to get but to give, one dedicated to God's glory and not to his own profit, one leading a life high in principle and pure in morals. The foreign missionary is America's finest ambassador.

But these missionaries do not ask admiration for their accomplishments any more than they ask sympathy for their sacrifices. What they do ask and want and need is, in brutal frankness, our help. This is funneled to them chiefly through the Pope's own Society for the Propagation of the Faith, which contributes to the support of some two hundred thousand bishops and priests, Sisters and Brothers, in the foreign mission field. Nevertheless, forty cents of every dollar donated in this country goes to *our needy home missions* in the United States, all the way from the deep South to the rugged Northwest.

As the lone foreign missionary jogs along in the saddle, with the sweat streaming down his face and steaming his sticky shirt, the hooves of his horses may pound out strange rhythms. I wonder: Does it ever seem to beat out, "Six to one, six to one, six to one"? This would not be the odds on a race but the lopsided figures on mission contributions. Or didn't you know that for every dollar that Catholics give to our missions, Protestants give six dollars to theirs?

Somehow, I think of Bishop Francis X. Ford of Maryknoll. His contribution to the foreign missions was his life. He came to China (by way of Brooklyn) back in 1918 when he was only a young priest of twenty-six. As a fellow Brooklynite I think of him whenever I go past King's Highway, which is a Brooklyn street and a subway stop. I wonder: Was he thinking of it, in the back of his holy head, when he wrote his little prayer, "Grant us, O Lord, to be the doorstep by which the multitudes may come to worship Thee. And if, in saving their souls, we are ground under foot and spat upon and worn out, we shall have become the King's Highway to pathless China."

In China, he was beloved by the common people and hated by the Communists who were then just coming into power. They bound his hands behind his back, paraded him through their territory, pelted him with stones, pounded him with clubs, and when he lay there in the mud, bruised and bleeding, they spat upon him and flung pails of garbage over his head. He died in 1952, in a Communist dungeon, as much a martyr as any Christian who perished under Nero.

The voice that calls us to help the Propagation of the Faith is the dying gasp of men like Bishop Ford. The hand into which we give our contribution is the scarlet, nail-pierced hand of Christ. If we listen to our own personal needs (we are all hard pressed), we shall never give much; but if we listen to the voice of men like Bishop Ford, if we look across the oceans into the hard and lonely spots where men like him are laboring now, we shall give from our heart.

Did you ever send a letter to yourself? Here is how you do it. Take a greenback, and some of us can make it a substantial greenback, fold it neatly, tuck it into the envelope tenderly, bid farewell to it fondly, seal it securely, send it to the Propagation of the Faith promptly, and some missionary will receive it gratefully.

How is it a letter to yourself? Well, they say that "you can't take it with you," but you can send it on ahead. And this is just what you will be doing. Someday, that letter will be waiting for you in the general post office of heaven.

Kindergarten Catholics

A silver-haired, silver-tongued salesman, who by that time was vice-president of his company, said to me after a sermon: "Father, never underestimate the intelligence of your audience, but never overestimate their information." The older I grow, the more I tend to agree, especially in the area of religion. This holds even for those who went to parochial schools or even Catholic high schools. At one time they knew precisely what was meant by the Incarnation or the Immaculate Conception, or a plenary indulgence or papal infallibility; but time has laid its layer of dull dust on what was once shining knowledge. For that matter, once they probably knew the exports of Ecuador, and the five causes of the American Civil War, and the six results of the Crusades, and simultaneous quadratic equations — but who would like to be interviewed on television about them now?

The sad fact is that in our learning days we probably also gave less time to religion than we gave to any other subject. In some Catholic schools, if the curriculum were a baseball team, religion would be the batboy; if it were a mansion, religion would be the broom closet. And even where it was given equal time, did we ever give the same preparation to religion as we gave to chemistry or mathematics? Religion? Why, we knew our religion! It just came to us, like breathing or chicken pox or a summer tan.

Besides, the chances are we learned our faith when our memory had muscles but our intelligence was mostly baby fat. We could reel off catechism questions and answers like coal rattling down a chute, but we did not fully understand their meaning. The Catholic faith we studied did not go through a thinking man's filter. Then, when our brain matured we never really went back, so that now on the keyboard of religion we don't dare go beyond a theological "I love coffee; I love tea."

Meanwhile the silt of secular knowledge settles upon us. As

149

a result, we get to know more about Grace Kelly than about sanctifying grace; more about mink stoles than about Mass stoles; more about money orders than holy orders; more about income tax than indulgences. Indulgences? An indulgence is something you take Alka-Seltzer for. Baseball players, movie stars, TV programs — all these we know; but our religion, beyond the rudimentary points of the compass, many of us do not know. We have oceans of knowledge about trivia and an eyedropperful of Christian doctrine.

Not that the aim is to become a parlor preacher or a tavern theologian — perish the thought! Deliver us from the loud, aggressive Catholic who all but grabs a stranger's lapels and asks if he does not want to hear a few good arguments in favor of the Catholic faith. Such a controversial Catholic who goes around with a chip on his shoulder (it probably fell there from his head) sets back ecumenism ten years every time he opens his belligerent mouth. Our religious knowledge should be a lamp to light with, not a lance to fight with.

On the other hand, nothing is more pathetic to the average non-Catholic than a Catholic who seems to believe so firmly but hardly knows why. It must be a headshaking marvel to such a one how an uninformed Catholic can follow the path of religion so blindly, led only by the Seeing Eye dog of faith. Our faith is not *that* blind! True, there are mysteries in the Catholic religion that the highest-powered telescope of human knowledge cannot fully reveal. This merely means that the creature can never know quite so much as his Creator. It does not take much humility or even logic to reconcile oneself to this.

Rather it recalls the incident of the kindergarten teacher who said, "Tommy, when you came into this warm classroom this morning you took off your overcoat. Now, if a polar bear came in, would it take off its big white furry coat too?" Tommy said, "No." The prodding teacher persisted, "But, why not?" "Because," answered Tommy, "only God knows where it is buttoned." Right; and only God knows where the mysteries are buttoned, and to us they must remain closed. But notice, our faith is blind only insofar as we cannot see how a certain situation can be. We are not blind as to what we believe or why we believe it. Basically, we believe because we take God's word. But in many matters there is much to *know*, if we only take the trouble to find out.

Certainly, Charlie Catholic makes a sorry figure if Bill Baptist or Pete Presbyterian asks him something about the Catholic Church and Charlie's knowledge at the moment is about as big as the olive drowning in his drink. It gets worse when he blusters and sputters in arguments that are all heat and no light, very loud but not very lucid. Someone has suggested that if you are a Catholic and do not know the answer, try to pretend that you are a visiting Muhammadan. But can you blame the inquiring non-Catholic for thinking (being perhaps much too polite to openly say so), "But you are a Catholic. This is your religion. You believe it. You are living your life by it. You are banking your eternity on it. And you don't seem to know anything about it."

In a sense it is flattering, because if you are a Catholic, they expect you to know. In other areas, ignorance is hardly noticed. In an election, a man may scarcely know the difference between a foreign policy and an insurance policy and still majestically cast a ballot that neutralizes the vote of a professor of political economy, a device that the good Lord possibly uses to make the miracle of democracy work. But in religion, if you do not know, they do not admire you for your simple faith but rather pity you for your stubborn foolishness.

If faith is a special gift of God, and it is, it flies on the flagstaff even above reason. But it does not contradict reason, and we need both. In a retreat house I used to watch a blind priest walk briskly from the chapel to the dining room without a cane. Between the chapel and the dining room ran a narrow strip of carpet across a hardwood floor. The old blind priest put one foot on the carpet, the other on the floor, and then walked straight as a major general on to his goal. Had he put both feet on the carpet, or both feet on the wooden floor there was no guide, and he could have ended up anywhere. But as long as that right foot was on the carpet and the left on the bare floor, his line was safe and straight.

In somewhat the same way, if we put one foot on the soft rug of faith and the other on the hard floor of reason, we walk safely too. Faith without reason can become wild superstition and reason without faith can become barren cynicism. But faith and reason together are the two arms of the great Gothic arch that points to God.

Because their forefathers were Catholics, many non-Catholics are instinctively curious about the Catholic faith, and if they can be shown that the Catholic faith is both faith and reason, like a bright statue set upon a cold marble pedestal, they will be attracted to it even more. Reason carries a man up to the threshold of the Church, and then faith stretches out its strong, unseen, heaven-sent hand and leads him across.

The Dove of the Holy Spirit never makes a forced landing, but in this matter of conversions, His descent is sometimes unpredictable and often astonishing. I know of a Catholic woman who once sent her neighbor, a fine Protestant woman who was a wheelchair invalid, a chicken pie. This was before our modern newfangled silver foil insulation; so she just wrapped it in the nearest paper at hand, which happened to be the Catholic diocesan weekly. The Protestant friend devoured both the pie and the paper. Something in the paper had appealed to her; she asked for other copies, and eventually came floating into the Church on the magic carpet of a Catholic paper.

Most conversions are a combination of information and inspiration. A gray-haired man attending the Funeral Mass of a priest was casually asked if he had known the deceased Father well. He shook his head. He was not a parishioner and had never met the dead priest in his life. "But," he said, "I often listened to him preach many years ago, during the First World War. I was not even a Catholic. I was a government agent who could speak German. This was then a German parish, and the priest had been reported for preaching anti-American sermons. So every Sunday I was told to sit in the pews and listen. I never heard one word against the American government, but every Sunday, I heard a fine little talk explaining some point of Catholic doctrine. It got me interested. I went to a priest in another parish and began to take instructions, and I have been a Catholic these many years. That's why I'm at the funeral this morning. The man who brought me into the Church never had the slightest idea what he was doing. But he knows now."

According to the Second Vatican Council, each of us, not just the clergy, is supposed to be an apostle. We are all commissioned to bring the good news of the true Church to our fellowmen. At least, we can be well enough informed on our faith to answer the ordinary questions. "Paperback" is a word that once had a bad name, but now there are all kinds of splendid paperbacks about the Church. There are pamphlets in parish racks on every conceivable topic. They cost a trifle and they teach the essentials, clearly and simply. A pamphlet can be theology without tears.

And as Cardinal Newman pleaded, "Give us a laity that is not brash, not arrogant, but a laity that knows its religion and enters into it, a laity that knows where it stands and what it holds, a laity that knows enough of faith to explain it and enough of history to defend it — God give us such an intelligent, well-informed laity!"

God give us? God help us to be! Or eventually, God help us!

PART **7**

spiritual nudges

Your Own Man (Or Woman)

If someone lays a heavy tip on a restaurant table, merely because he has been intimidated by the waiter, or because he wants to impress other diners, the moralists put him down as a victim of *human respect*. It is a curious phrase, that, because we never allude to the fear of God as divine respect, do we? But whether the phrase be curious or not, the line of conduct is common. How many people walk through the world looking over their shoulder and wondering and worrying what other people may be thinking about them! It is a pity too because, what is the point in giving so much attention to the rearview mirror when all progress and most danger lie up front?

The saints merely shrugged holy shoulders at the passing judgments of men. They were too deeply concerned with the ultimate judgment of God. They knew that you have about as much chance of escaping criticism as you have of avoiding colds. Do what you will, the bugs (and the brickbats) are going to come. Nobody is healthy all the time, and nobody is popular all the time. Everyone is at least the occasional target of rash judgments, which are so often wrong judgments. Even the good Lord could not please everybody. Ask Pilate or Herod or the money changers in the temple.

Scripture tells us they watched Him . . . watched Him with narrow, jealous eyes. They whispered about Him with bitter, scathing tongues. Should Christians hope for better treatment than Christ? Since when is the disciple above the Master?

Look at the record. When Jesus reached out His kindly hand and almost casually cured the sick, they denounced Him for doing it on the Sabbath. When He sat down to eat in the house of Zacchaeus, the tax gatherer, and when He granted forgiveness to Mary Magdalene, the woman of ill-repute, they condemned Him for associating with sinners. When He drew large crowds by going about doing good, they accused Him of disturbing the peace. When He preached the Good News of the kingdom of heaven, they spread the word that He was leading a revolution against the kingdom of Caesar. When He dazzled them with an outpouring of miracles like an exploding display of fireworks (helpless cripples leaped up and the raging storm lay down, bread multiplied and water blushed into wine, blind men saw and dead men flung aside their funeral shrouds) — when they could not deny this parade of marvels and could not hush the telling, they hinted that He was in league with the devil, and *that* was the whole explanation of how He worked such wonders.

Why then should we, as Christians, complain about what others may think or say about us, when the same thing happened to our Leader, Christ? Should it not rather assure us that we are on the right path, the path that He plodded before us, with all its sharp stones, its jagged chips of glass, its slimy mud puddles?

As long as human nature endures, human beings will be mentally judging (or misjudging) and verbally criticizing other human beings. The only way to escape being a target is to be insignificant. But to be ignored is perhaps a greater hurt than to be denounced. It is the ultimate scorn.

Would you not rather hold up a soaring spire than be an underground cave? Be a cathedral rather than a catacomb? The bear who could spend his whole life in sleepy hibernation would never come within range of the hunter's gun, but would you call it life? In both the physical and the moral world, activity invites risk.

Have you ever wondered what it is in us that makes us so prone to dissect another's character under the lens of the microscope, or to follow his actions with a spyglass? Some thoughtful men believe that the answer lies in another kind of glass: a mirror. In our neighbor we see ourselves.

We know what is written in our own diary, and we would like to believe that the same smudgy pages exist in his too. More than fifteen centuries ago Saint John Chrysostom (the name means "golden mouth," but "steel-edged tongue" might have described him better) said, "You suspect your brother's action only because you feel in yourself the same evil inclinations that you think you see in him." Note, though, how carefully the saint slides in his stiletto, making the sharp distinction between what we are sure of in ourselves and what we would like to suspect in another.

In practice it can come out something like this. A quiet man of deep courage may be patiently enduring an unjust situation, but because he does not scream protests, we put him down as timid and afraid. Why? Because *we* are timid and afraid. A woman may be pious and prayerful, but we put her down as a hypocrite because we find prayer a bore. Those who are truly conscientious we put down as scrupulous, because *we* tend to be lax and to take moral corners with a wide swing. We shake our heads at someone's interest in church activities, affairs and general dedication to religion as being fanatical, because our own attitude is indifferent or cold.

But no matter the reason why we X-ray the actions and motives of others, this particular type of X ray is not painless. It can hurt. Everybody talks about constructive criticism but much criticism only destroys. It is like the huge iron wrecking ball that pounds the building to rubble.

Knowing this, it takes more than an eyedropperful of courage to be the person we should be, to say the things we should say, and to do the things we should do, even when we know we offer ourselves like Saint Sebastian as the target for the arrows of demeaning slurs. One small example: In a crowd, try to stop the air pollution of dirty stories and see what happens. They will give you a halo and pull it down over your eyes.

On the head of the Sovereign Pontiff there sits a white skullcap known as a "Soli Deo" (Latin for "Only to God"). The Pope removes this only at the Consecration of the Mass . . . only to God. Every Christian's soul should wear one too, reminding him that he must never yield to the pressure of mere men.

There is always the danger that the taunts of men can drown out the voice of God. Here is where singleness of purpose has to win the day. Even in the material world that quality is respected. There comes to mind the incident of Czar Nicholas I and the railroad he decided to build nearly one hundred fifty years ago. The engineers spread out their plans, revealing a twisting, winding route that coiled like a writhing snake between Moscow and old St. Petersburg, which is now Leningrad. It seems that wily Russian nobles had bribed the surveyors to bring the railroad near their farms and estates.

The czar looked at the plans, scowled and flung them on the floor, thundering: "Bring me a map of Russia." He set the map on the table, took a ruler, laid one end at Moscow, the other at St. Petersburg, drew a straight direct line, and tersely said, "Build your railroad there!" And today that railroad runs four hundred four miles in an almost perfect, unwavering line.

If you do your duty, you dare not swerve. You cannot compromise. You will not go around. You must go straight on. Again, Saint Paul: "If I please only men, I shall not be the servant of Jesus Christ."

"What will people think?" Our Lady herself must have wondered that before the Virgin Birth. How many hours of agony did she endure till the angel assured Joseph that the Holy Spirit had overshadowed her and that her unborn Child would be the Son of God!

We, to be sure, have more prosaic problems. But the principle is the same. A man is a fool if he goes through life worrying about what people may be thinking. It does not matter in the least what anybody thinks if we know that we are following our conscience.

Not far from where this is being written Wendell Phillips dared to speak out a century ago for the rights of the black man to an audience that took slavery for granted. He left that hall under police escort and, even so, was pelted with filth and threatened with violence right up to his doorstep. The newspapers, the state legislature, the Protestant clergy (there were no Catholics to speak of) were all against him. But he would not be silenced. He marched to his own drummer. Today there rises in his memory an almost apologetic belated statue.

So, too, many of the saints walked alone in a world that either hated them or pitied them. The moral still holds: It does not matter a whit what people think; what does matter is what God knows. And God knows a man should follow his own conscience even if he has to walk alone!

Living the Faith

The musical "Godspell" sent ringing over the footlights the information that "gospel" meant "good news." If so, then the priest who preaches the Good News is a kind of press agent, a press agent of God. But if that is the case, we priests are doing a rather indifferent job. We surely have not launched a very successful public relations campaign to make people conscious of how important God and His Gospel are.

Poll the traditional "average man in the street." Ask him what's on his mind at the moment. He may tell you it is some sticky problem on the job, or a child sick at home, or even perhaps the latest political scandal. But you would almost have to buttonhole a monk to get an answer with the slightest over-tone of religion.

Religion? The average Catholic treats his religion like his newspaper. He is willing to give it a glance in the morning (a quick, yawning, mumbled prayer), another longer glance in the evening (night prayers) and a larger edition on the weekend (Sunday Mass). But by and large his religion rolls along as aimlessly as a newspaper page blown along a windy street. It has no particular purpose, no concern, no deep vital interest.

He wears his faith, to put it another way, like the old red cassock of the altar boy in the country mission church. On Sundays and holy days the cassock comes out of the closet for an hour or so, and then goes back to the dust and the moths for the rest of the week.

So little of our faith gets into our gut, into our attitudes, into our values, into the nitty-gritty of our daily decisions, our character, our daily life. Do we, for example, who treat religion so routinely, ever regard the gift of faith as the tremendous treasure it is, the pearl of great price, the key of heaven? Do we hold it above all else in this cheap and tawdry world? Answer: We rarely even think of it. (In this blunt questionnaire your reaction may be the utter opposite. I had the disadvantage of interviewing only a mirror.)

Take just one digit on the great round dial of faith, the Blessed Sacrament. Does this breathtaking wonder ever awe us, that Jesus Christ is as truly present behind the golden door of the tabernacle as He ever was in the yellow straw of the manger? Answer: We rarely advert to it.

Or consider sin. Does the deep, diabolical evil of serious sin, its brazen rebellion against our Creator, its slimy treason against our Redeemer — does this ever sadden us or disgust us, or even just bother us? Answer: We almost dismiss sin with a shrug.

Does the rumbling thunder of the eternal truths ever terrify us? The certain, grim fact, for instance, that at the end of our

159

earthly road there gapes an open grave, with Death like a grinning skeleton leaning on his shovel, waiting, waiting? No matter what may have happened in the play of life, this is the last scene of the last act. Does this make us bite our lips and stare into space? Answer: We manage to think of something else.

And the sequel, for death is only the dark drapery before the hall of judgment — does that disturb us, or distress us, or send us searching down into the cellar of our soul? Answer: Switch to another channel, or turn the TV up louder.

Perhaps we console ourselves that when it comes to the basics we are, after all, of the Catholic faith, and our name is written large in some baptismal register. But if shrouds don't have pockets, caskets don't have places for baptismal registers either.

The Catholic, incidentally, who boasts beyond measure of his baptism, is sometimes that curious kind of Catholic who is either a "born" Catholic or a "snob" Catholic. The "born" Catholic looks down a pious, pitying nose on the "convert" Catholic as a second-class Johnny-come-lately. The "snob" Catholic resents the fact (and it is a fact) that there are so many Catholics who are "ethnics" — that is, Italians or French-Canadians or Portuguese or Irish or Puerto Ricans.

Pray that such a snob Catholic is not also a lukewarm or borderline Catholic, the sad type about which a Catholic admiral, speaking to midshipmen at a Communion breakfast many years ago, said: "Some Catholic officers give up their faith for one gold stripe, and some for two."

This is the kind of freewheeling Catholic who takes his theology on birth control not from the Pope, the successor of Saint Peter, but from some maverick curate in North Overshoe, South Dakota, who at the moment would rather see his picture in the newspaper than his name in the *Book of Life*.

When you come down to it, the Grand Canyon of difference between a genuine Catholic and a counterfeit Catholic is the huge chasm between motions and motives. The counterfeit Catholic just goes through the ritual motions. The genuine Catholic is fueled by his motives, his deep, inner, religious convictions. How can anyone resist the mighty, modern temptations all around him unless he has even stronger spiritual convictions within him?

To live up to the Catholic faith you must first love the faith. To be loyal to the faith you must treasure it above all else. True, a man must make a living, but he should never be so involved in making a living that he forgets the goal of eternal life. Just as sunglasses give the world a different tint, so "soul glasses" present the world in a different shade.

On all this earth there is but one central figure, one towering person, the Savior who hung from the autumn-red tree of the cross. The ABC's of life are to follow in His footsteps, to hear and heed His words. He left us His laws to keep, His sacraments to strengthen, His presence to comfort. The rest is peanut shells.

True, we do have free will; so if we choose, we can break His laws like peanut brittle. But if we defiantly do, we are damned. This, of course, is fire-and-brimstone religion, which the sophisticated will smilingly dismiss. They would prefer a religion (as who would not?) of lavender and old rose and the organ playing softly at twilight. The golden rule (they say) is religion enough, thank you, the way He presented it in the Sermon on the Mount. But are they not forgetting that in this same Sermon on the Mount the gentle Christ made five separate references to hell?

They would much prefer (and who would not, if there were a choice?) to turn their thoughts away from hell to someone like Saint Francis. Ah, Saint Francis, that dear, vivacious little man, with the thick black hair and the soft brown eyes and the monk's gray hood, singing down the highway of history, with the flowers nodding as he passed, and birds perching upon his shoulders like epaulets.

This Saint Francis might easily be mistaken for the head of the Garden Clubs of America, or president of the National Society of Birdwatchers. Believe me, he was not canonized for this.

It grows the more confusing when you ponder his famous prayer laminated on so many pious plaques: "Lord, make me an instrument of your peace; ... where there is darkness, [let me sow] light." But the darkness he had in mind was the darkness of pagan unbelief, which is why he marched off to preach the Gospel to infidels. "Where there is doubt, [let me sow] faith." The only faith he was concerned with was the only faith he ever knew, the faith as believed and practiced in his Catholic Church. Saint Francis heard its Mass, received its Holy Communion, obeyed its Pope, preached its doctrines, and when he was dying at Assisi (blindly blessing the monks he could not see), received its last sacraments. When his hands stiffened in death lay outstretched, they were scarred with the stigmata of Calvary's nails, to remind the doubtful that it is not an easy thing to follow Christ and His holy way.

If Saint Francis should return, he might be astonished at all the Christian Churches that lift separate steeples in one town. But he would seek out the Church he remembered. It is probable that some of the changes inside the stained-glass windows might cause his dark eyebrows to arch in mild wonder and even draw forth a soft pious whistle. But he would soon discover that it was only the tassels and the fringes that had been changed. The fabric — consisting of the unchanging fundamentals — was still as it always had been.

He would find there is still One God, still Three Persons, still Four Gospels, still Seven Sacraments, still Ten Commandments. There is still the Mass and still Mary, still the Pope and still purgatory, still heaven and hell.

But with all today's vague, wishy-washy propaganda (or improperganda) he might find it even more difficult to become a saint.

Beyond the Church Doors

Somewhere during the Easter season there is a prayer in the liturgy that stands, like a bugler on a parapet, and announces the duty of Christians so clearly that it startles. The prayer goes like this, "O Lord, grant that our actions may reflect what our words proclaim." You can't get it much blunter or straighter than that, can you? That brief petition certainly presents something to think about as a motto, or better, to march behind like a banner, each time service is over and we go out beyond the church doors into the practical world. That particular service is over: We have served the Lord. Now is the time to think about serving our fellowman, and fulfilling the awesome, monumental command of loving our neighbor as ourselves.

In various eras of history, Christianity had to live in a sheltered cocoon of isolation and secrecy. During the bloody persecutions of the Roman Empire, the Church crouched in the underground shadows of the catacombs. During the Dark Ages, when the barbarians wanted to leave civilization a charred path in their wake, monks like Saint Columba of Iona kept both the altar light of faith and the lamp of learning burning brightly in remote monasteries. Just to survive, the Church had to stay far away from the conflicts of the world.

In a somewhat similar way and for similar reasons, the Catholics of the United States had to stay by themselves during the last century. They huddled together in their own little parish — call it a Catholic ghetto or a fortress of the faith. You could hardly blame them, because they were, in the vast majority, recent immigrants to America and the only place where they felt at home was the Church.

It did not matter whether they came from Italy or from Ireland, from Germany or Poland or French Canada, they felt comfortable because the altar and the statues and the Latin Mass were the same as at home. Confession and Communion, the way

163

of the cross, the rosary — it was not only their childhood religion, it was their spiritual security blanket, their assurance that despite this strange new world all was safe and well.

Later on, when bigotry reared its slashing head they retreated even deeper into the enclave of their Catholic parish, Catholic customs, Catholic neighbors. In New England, signs appeared in store windows: MAN WANTED — NO CATHOLIC NEED APPLY. In the South and in the Midwest, the Ku Klux Klan burned crosses on the lawns of Catholic churches. In general, Catholics were looked down upon, because they were poor and uneducated, and considered good for nothing but maidservants and stablemen for the well-to-do. Is it any wonder (since the only thing Catholics could esteem was their faith) that the Catholic Church in the United States just gritted its teeth, and lived by itself, and tried to survive as a tiny Catholic island in a vast non-Catholic and often anti-Catholic sea?

Thank God, this hostile horizon has now receded, and for decades Catholics have been accepted as ordinary members of the community. This means that we no longer have an excuse to stay inside a Catholic ghetto, because the day of the Catholic ghetto is gone. Now we have not only the opportunity but the obligation to leave our citadel of truth and march out among all people and let the Church make its impact on them.

But to do this we must live among our non-Catholic neighbors as Catholics who live their faith and show the fruit of that faith in their lives. We cannot expect to influence people if we wander among them as cold, legalistic religionists. We cannot expect our neighbors to listen to cocktail homilies or laymen's sermons. We have to be kindly and outgoing and compassionate. The world will not be converted by the cold logic of Catholicism as much as by the warm friendliness of Catholics. First we must be openhearted and sympathetic and deeply concerned about the problems of others.

Piety is fine, but practical charity is even better. There are

Catholics, good devout Catholics, who drop into church often, say the beads daily, receive Communion frequently, even make the stations regularly — but their religion stops there. They are like a tight little bud on a rosebush caught in a frost. The bud never expands, never unfolds, never flings the fragrance of its goodness round about. Such a bud vividly portrays the difference between a hand rigidly clasped in selfishness and a hand stretched out in generous help, between religion that is self-centered and religion that reaches out toward its neighbor.

A Catholic who goes to church week after week or even day after day and does not let his fervor overflow toward his fellow-man in friendly kindness and even material help is like a man who spends a lifetime in college, always learning and never leaving and never achieving anything. This is keeping the Catholic faith walled up in a tomb instead of bringing it out into the marketplace. If now we are able to come out of the Catholic ghetto, in God's name, let us come out! We shall not be shortchanging God or weakening the faith. Rather we are living it, taking it out of the catechism and bringing it to the sidewalk and the living room and the office and the hospital.

Even the strictest Catholic theologians agree that it is better to miss Mass if you miss it because you have to take care of someone who is sick. This is in line with our Lord's warning that at the last judgment the test will be serving our neighbor. "Because you saw me hungry and fed me, naked and you clothed me, in prison and you visited me. . . ." And our bewildered question, "But, Lord, when did we see you hungry or naked or in prison?" And the amazing answer: "As long as you did it to the least of these my brethren, you did it to me."

Our gentle Savior rarely used irony but I think he flashed it in the parable of the Good Samaritan. There he shows us the wounded traveler, robbed of his money, stripped of his robe, bleeding in the dust. Then Christ pointedly says that a priest from the temple saw him, and passed by. After him, a Levite, next in rank at the temple to the priests, saw him and also passed by. But a Samaritan saw him and stopped. Samaritan! To the Jews a Samaritan was a heretic, a half-breed, an outcast, the scum of the earth. But this was the man who stopped; this was the man who delayed his own journey and did something practical. This man, rather than priest or Levite, will hear the heavenly call of Christ, "Come, you blessed of my Father!"

The road on which the episode happened ran down between Jerusalem and Jericho. The same road in a Christian sense still runs through every city and small town of America. For that reason, we should ask ourselves: Are we perhaps passing someone by, someone whom we should now be helping? I think of fathers working two jobs in order to survive in this richest nation in the world. I think of mothers struggling with all the cares of a large family. I think of young people trying to work their way through college. I think of patients in hospitals where the mere thought of the bill is enough to make them sick again. I think of children in institutions, who are not available for adoption, but who do need and crave a foster home.

And how about the civil rights of our neighbors? Deep down do we believe that some people, like blacks or Puerto Ricans or Mexicans or Indians, are second-class citizens — like the Irish a hundred years ago? Surely there are thieves and villains among them (as among us all), but do we judge them as we should, not as a group, but individual for individual, and thereby encourage them to climb to the plateau where they ought to be?

This does not mean that we stop being Catholics and become members of the Welfare Department or the Salvation Army or the Red Cross. It does not mean that we should go to church less. In fact the more we do go to church, the broader will be the branches and the richer the fruit of the tree of our charity. Love of neighbor at its finest is rooted in love of God, who is the Father of us all. And each of us is His child.

PART **8**

Marian bouquet

The King's Candle

If you ask the average literate Catholic to name England's
most famous shrine he would probably name Canterbury, the cathedral where Saint Thomas à Becket fell in a scarlet pool of
martyr's blood. Who has not heard of Chaucer's garrulous pilgrims — the nun and the knight and the parson, and the generally rowdy rest? With their swaying horses and earthy tales they
still ride across the horizon of literature as fascinating and unfor-
gettable characters. In fact, does not that very word "canter"
come right out of Canterbury, coined to describe the unhurried
gait of the pilgrim's horse en route to the shrine?

But a strong contender for honors (at least in history if not
in poetry) was a gray abbey that rose out of the green fields of
Norwich called Our Lady of Walsingham. England had long
been called "Our Lady's Dowry," and to this Marian shrine for
unnumbered years there came in devout pilgrimage commoners,
cardinals, kings, to pray before the famous image of Mary carved
out of oak.

Curiously enough, the last king to kneel there was Henry
VIII. Since he was then still married to his first wife, Katherine
of Aragón, we should presume that he was as sincere as any other
pilgrim.

That was in the bitter winter of 1521. True, Henry had rid-
den or rattled to Walsingham in his gilded coach, but two miles
from the shrine he ordered the coach to stop. Off came the royal

boots and the warm woolen socks, and for the rest of the way over January's ice and snow he trudged barefoot. When he had crossed himself and said his prayers before the dark statue, he lit what amounted to a king-size votive light. It was a candle tall as the king himself. Further, he gave orders that when it had burned down, another like it must be lit to symbolize that no matter where he might be in body, in spirit he was always at Walsingham, kneeling before our Lady's shrine. "The king's candle must never go out!"

Henry left and never returned. It was a dramatic gesture, of course, this bit about the king's candle; but the externals of piety are only as good as the internal resolution, the dedication of the heart, just as paper dollars are good only if backed up by the solid gold bars in Fort Knox. Apparently the king changed. Thereafter, out of the frame of any page of history his portrait shows the merry monarch, the lusty, gusty Henry the Eighth. But "monarch" literally means one who governs by himself. Henry could not govern even himself.

From the time he turned his eyes away from the immaculate Lady of Walsingham, those eyes turned lecherous, and roved toward other ladies far from immaculate. Then began that tragic procession of a half-dozen wives, half of whom marched from Henry's silken pillow to the hard and splintery pillow of the headsman's block. But Henry did not altogether forget Walsingham. He remembered it when he needed funds. He sent his henchmen to loot the shrine.

First they murdered, or in God's eyes they martyred, the five monks who staffed the abbey. Then they proceeded to strip (with the connivance of a bribed abbot) the very walls of the thanksgiving offerings that grateful pilgrims had left. Henry's minions took gold, jewels — everything and anything of value. Finally they dragged down the oak statue of our Lady and eventually it became the core of a sacrilegious bonfire. The flames leaped high, then gradually fell away to glowing pink embers and flaked into gray ashes. Now at last the king's candle was forever out, and in more than one sense, darkness came down over Walsingham like a lid laid on a coffin.

For centuries England's most famous shrine has stood in those silent fields as a roofless ruin, an abandoned altar, high broken arches through whose ivy the wind playfully rippled and through whose empty gaping windows the birds streaked and dipped in careless flight. A great lonely tombstone of the faith.

Weep, weep, O Walsingham,
*   Whose days are nights:*
Blessings turned to blasphemies,
*   Holy deeds to despites;*
Sin is where our Lady sat;
*   Heaven turned to hell:*
Satan sits where our Lord did sway —
*   Walsingham, oh, farewell.*

You can forsake the Mother of God. You can forget her. You can (in a dictator role) forbid other people to honor her. But you can never bury her. Her assumption into heaven proved that. How often bigotry's persecution is like a cloud that temporarily obscures the moon. For a short while the moon seems lost; but the cloud turns out to have been only a ragged chamois cloth that has polished the moon into a gleaming silver tray, brighter than before.

History can tell of times when the very stones that had battered down our Lady's image were gathered up by a repentant posterity and piled up to build a pedestal for the triumphant return of the new Madonna.

Take Walsingham, where the pilgrims have begun to return. There is even a place along the road called the Slipper Chapel where the more devout remove their shoes and plod the last two miles barefoot. But the main point is that they pray the old prayers, sing the old hymns, paying honor once more to the not-old but the ever-young Mary, Our Lady of Walsingham.

If the poet could "weep, weep for Walsingham," would not a saint pity those who gave up an early devotion to God's Mother? Henry VIII is a sorry example. As long as we have temptations that tap at our elbows, problems that press in around us, sorrows that darken the doorway of our life, we need Mary and the special help that she can win us from her Son. Let our love for our Lady be not like the king's candle that so soon guttered out, but burn like the fire in a ruby — glowing quietly, glowing constantly, a flame that never dies!

Mary, Candlestick of Christ

I have always admired, this side of adulation, the loyal old guard, those lovers of our Lady who put in a faithful appearance, week after week, at the so-called perpetual novenas. Granted that they may be asking personal help in this area or that; at least they recognize that perpetual help on Mary's part implies and entails perpetual devotion on theirs.

The opposite to this is that type of person who loves our Lady for a little while and then casually leaves her. Such devotion is a fire of straw. Ever see a bundle of straw touched with a match? It leaps up hissing and sizzling and crackling into a brave flame, and then, even as you watch, drops away to a black and charred nothingness. Why not? There was never any solid fuel to sustain it. And so with a certain class of people: Their devotion is all enthusiasm and no conviction. It is only sentiment without a solid spiritual base.

Certainly, our devotion to Mary should be enthusiastic and warm and ardent; it should be like one of those gorgeous statues of the Madonna, all gaily tinted and brightly gilded, but set upon a pedestal of solid marble. So our devotion to Mary, however fervent it may be, should rest upon premises of cold, solid logic.

Why, then, do we honor Mary and invoke her? We might start way back and figure it this way. All that we have, we have obviously from God. But God gives us nothing directly. His long arm does not stretch out of the sky and present us with this or that. If He wants to give us rain, He sends the gray, rolling cloud-ships to unload their streaming cargo. If He wants to give us light, He does it through the golden lamp of the sun. And if He wants to give us grace (either temporal help or spiritual), He does it through the Mass, through the sacraments, through answered prayer, and (what concerns us here) through the intercession of His Mother.

But how, precisely, does Mary send us grace? In our rude human way of computing, the Savior merited His infinite graces for us by being born among us, living with us and dying for us. But in each of these areas, His closest cooperator was Mary, His Mother.

When He was born at Bethlehem — in that original Christian catacomb, that rocky cave, that first chapel of the world, where the golden tabernacle was golden straw and the sanctuary lamp was a flaming star — who was it that laid Him in the manger? Who but Mary, His Mother?

When He lived among us, in that quaint and quiet village of Nazareth (which to Jesus was "Home, Sweet Home"), who was it that guided Him in His toddling baby days, brought Him up through slender, bronze-limbed boyhood, reared Him even into strong and stalwart manhood — who was it but Mary, His Mother?

And when He finally died at Calvary on that awesome day when the sky was black and the cross was bloody, when they had spread His young body out on the gibbet as crudely and as cruelly as if they were stretching out the skin of an animal to dry, whose heart was it that felt every blow of the hammer, whose heart became a crimson pincushion for every prodding thorn,

171

whose love made her stay there beneath the cross, loyal to the last, when the Apostles had taken to their cowardly heels — who was there to comfort and console to the very end but Mary, His Mother?

And precisely because Mary was so close to Christ at the crib of Bethlehem, so close to Him in the cottage at Nazareth, so close to Him under the cross of Calvary, this is precisely why we believe that she is so close to His throne in heaven. This is why we believe that Mary has such gentle, persuasive power over Jesus. This is why we do not hesitate to ask her to be our powerful intercessor at His throne.

Does it not seem logical? If God gave us His most precious gift, His only Son, through Mary (He was the fruit of her womb) why should He not give us lesser gifts through Mary, as the fruit of her petition? If, in God's eyes, Mary was good enough to be the means of giving us the Savior, why should she not also be the channel through which He can, when He wishes, give us the means of salvation?

In a homely comparison this is like the situation that prevails in the ordinary family. Who earns the family's daily bread? Ordinarily, the man of the house. But who distributes it to the children? The mother. In like manner, our blessed Lord has merited all the graces and blessings for humankind, but often He distributes them through His Mother, as shrines like Lourdes and LaSalette and Guadalupe and Fatima gloriously attest.

Or perhaps Mary's role can be brought out better through another illustration. Many years ago, in the days when irrigation was primitive, settlers in some parts of the Far West found that the land was parched as powder. But up above this dry earth loomed hills dotted with shining lakes. So the settlers would dig a channel straight up the hillside, clear to the brim of the lake. Alongside this channel they ran a telephone line. Then, in the spring, when the lake was foaming with melted mountain snow, while the earth below was crumbling-dry, they would phone up,

"Open this sluice! Open that sluice!" And the water came rushing and gushing down to the fields below. The land was made moist and rich and fertile, and some of the finest fruit was raised in that region.

So you see the picture? There is our blessed Savior up there (as we crudely say) with a bottomless and boundless reservoir of graces that He merited by His life and sufferings and death. And here are we, needing graces, pleading for graces, parched for graces. And in between is Mary. She is both the telephone line that carries our call for help up to Jesus, and the channel that brings down His graces and helps and gifts to us.

The obvious objection to this, of course, is the question, "Why can we not go to our Savior directly?" And the answer is that we can go, and often do so, as we should. In every perpetual novena to our Lady that I have seen, the prayers to our Lady were joined either to a Mass or Benediction, and certainly the Mass and Benediction are directed only to Christ.

However, there are moments in the lives of most of us when we feel unworthy to approach that great God, when we are overwhelmed with our sense of guilt, heartsick at sins of the past. Then, as we crawl along the muddy ground of our remorse, we reach out to clutch the spotless robe of the Immaculate Mary, and beg her to intercede in our behalf. Or we may desperately want this or that from God, but we know in our guilty hearts that we do not deserve it, so we ask our Lady, His Mother, to plead our cause.

In this we are backed up historically by the wedding feast of Cana. Remember, up to that event, Mary had never seen a miracle. Up to that time Christ had never performed a miracle. In the circumstances there seemed no call for a miracle. Here were just a couple of newlyweds who were embarrassed because their wedding reception had run out of refreshments. Hardly an earth-shaking catastrophe demanding the intervention of the miraculous! And yet our Lord, to show His love for His Mother, to show her sweet and powerful influence over Him, to show how He answered her prayer, performed then and there an utterly unscheduled wonder, changing the water into wine.

Perhaps that is why in every Catholic church you will find an image of Mary. That church is not a bleak house, missing a mother's love, but like the cottage where Jesus lived at Nazareth, Mary is there, the lady of the house.

About a hundred years ago an Anglican clergyman was plodding through the hills of Sicily when he was suddenly overtaken by a summer storm. The nearest shelter was the arched entrance of a little stone church. He huddled there for a while but then the pelting rain forced him inside. In the semidarkness he made out near the altar a marble statue of the Madonna, with a single candle flickering before it. Outside, the skies blackened, the storm roared, the rain sluiced down, the lightning lit up the stained-glass windows. Inside he found himself in deep, prayerful peace.

After a long while he came out. The sky was clear, the sun was gold again, the gloom and the turmoil gone. He never forgot that image of Mary nor the candle with its white beam shining on it. Already in his mind he was thinking of the hymn he would write, "Lead, kindly light, amid the encircling gloom! Lead Thou me on!"

That Light eventually led the Anglican clergyman into the Catholic Church where he became the celebrated Cardinal Newman.

Spiritual Service Station

Our blessed Lord spoke from some strange pulpits, but whether He was preaching from the green summit of a Galilean hill or the lapping prow of Peter's boat, He used language and illustrations that His hearers were sure to understand. Since it was a first-century audience, the examples were drawn from first-century life. To us who live in the twentieth century many of our Lord's references are remote and quaint and known only through pictures. When, for example, was the last time you actually saw a millstone, or a mustard seed, or a yoke of plowing oxen, or a wine flask made of skin, or even a huge net thrashing with silver fish?

If our Savior were addressing a modern audience, His speech would be sprinkled with allusions to modern times. The lessons would be drawn not from lost sheep or lepers or fig trees or widow's mites but from tractors and cellophane and penicillin and jet planes and filling stations.

Let's stop there, at the filling station. We generally do, don't we? Besides, all the foregoing has been a sneaky way of presenting what some may consider an extravagant idea — that is, the shrine of our Lady and the weekly novena in her honor is like a spiritual filling station.

Such a theme may send some pious eyebrows up in uneasy wonder, but there are points worth considering. No motorist, to begin with, swings into a filling station just to be at the filling station. We drive to the ball park for the sake of the ball game, but we do not go to the filling station for the sake of the filling station, but rather with an eye to the long hard miles ahead. As a matter of fact, if there is one time when we do not need gas or oil, it is precisely while we are sitting there at the filling station. It is only when we leave the filling station that the good of it begins to take effect. More than that. Though we may leave the filling station, it does not really leave us, because part of it goes with us, and helps us up every steep hill and around every curling road till we reach our destination.

Isn't this the same way with a weekly novena service? We are there not merely for the sake of that half hour. We are fueling up with grace for all the half hours that lie ahead during the week. We are preparing ourselves spiritually to encounter the many problems and the various people that lie between us and our next visit to the shrine. *Then* is when we shall need the grace of God to act like children of God! The truth is that (as at the filling station) we never need God's grace less than during the half hour we devoutly spend at the novena service. We are in God's house. We are not yet in enemy country. It is only when the last note of the last hymn has trailed off, when the golden gleam of the monstrance has been reposed like a setting sun, when the people pour out like a bobbing, colorful stream — it is only then that the benefits of the service (or the spiritual service station) begin to register. We leave now with new moral fuel, with the gauge of grace in our soul reading FULL. How necessary this is, only the Lord knows, since only He knows what rough road may lie before us in the week ahead, and how many times we shall need that full tank of high-powered grace!

Isn't it always prudent, too, to provide for emergencies? We do it in other areas; why not in our spiritual life also? In a hospital if a person needs blood before or after an operation, there is the blood bank, ready to supply a rich, life-saving transfusion. If another patient, with chest heaving, gasps hungrily for air, there is the oxygen, either wheeled in by tank or piped in from the wall. But whether it is a matter of blood bank or oxygen tank, we have a vivid example of how the reserves come through in a crisis and how a supply stored up can save the day.

Such is the case when the body hovers between life and death, and such is also the case when the soul hovers between virtue and sin. Whether we then feebly give in, or whether we gallantly hold out, may well depend on whether we have the extra grace in reserve to give the extra moral strength we need. On the military scene where armies are locked in swaying combat, how often a cloud of dust on the horizon has announced the arrival of fresh troops and a sudden victory! On the battlefield of the soul it happens the same way. To us, fighting wearily and all but giving up, suddenly out of nowhere will come riding a column of grace that was gained in months of devotion at our Lady's shrine.

Someone has written a fiercely pleading prayer that has been set to an impassioned ringing hymn: "Lord, for tomorrow and its needs I do not pray. Keep me from stain of sin just for today!" Good enough. That is, the sentiment is good and the prayer is enough. Enough for the ordinary day when ordinary prayer will obtain ordinary grace to conquer ordinary temptations or to endure ordinary trials. But who knows what tragic tomorrows lie ahead, like long black tunnels, through which we shall have to pass before we come out again into the serene sunlight of peace and joy?

Who dares predict what may lie under the next thin leaf of the calendar? Who can foretell through what numbered square pale sickness may break through to touch us with its gaunt finger, or black bereavement to hang its crepe upon our heart, or gray disappointment to swirl its bleak clouds around some golden dream? Who knows the sorrow of tomorrow or the staggering blow of next week?

All this may seem a bit morbid, almost like trying to lift up a dark corner of the future and trying to peer in. Certainly, smooth diplomacy or Pollyannaish Christianity would never risk it. But faith is not afraid. We know that this world can never be heaven, that it is only a testing ground for heaven, and that at some time or another it becomes for most of us what the prayer to our Lady calls, "this vale of tears." Not that we should brood over the future, but at least we should be prepared, and the best way to be prepared is to be pre-prayered.

That is why those who are regular attendants at a novena in honor of Mary, our blessed Mother, should find deep and warm comfort in the knowledge that with every service they attend, with every hymn they sing, with every prayer they say, they are not only laying up for themselves treasures in heaven, but are also strengthening their moral muscles here on earth. To put it another way, the novena service of Tuesday will help you conquer the temptation of Wednesday or to carry the unexpected cross of Thursday. You are preparing for the possible sorrow of tomorrow by the novena devotion of today.

It is worthwhile to remember this when it seems hard to come to the services. We hail Mary as full of grace, and she is the only creature that ever was. The rest of us need grace direly, and one of the finest channels of grace is the weekly service at her shrine. Without grace our spiritual life withers. It may not be evident on the outside, but the slow silent dying goes on. In a way it resembles a plane flying over a gorgeous New England landscape in gay October. The land rolls under the plane like a rich Oriental rug. A stand of scarlet maples blazes like a silent forest fire. A solitary elm lifts its lacy golden leaves like a delicate filigreed monstrance.

But don't let it fool you. Underneath all this splendor is the beginning of seasonal death. The source of life has been shut off. No longer does the bubbling sap shoot up the tree trunk like an elevator, and then stream out over a network of arteries through every branch to the last topmost trembling leaf. The vital nourishment has been stopped at its source and soon those leaves shrivel up and spiral giddily down, till there stands only the black-ribbed skeleton of a tree, waiting for the spring to sound its trumpet for resurrection.

The soul that is dead is like a dark November wasteland. The soul that is alive is green and growing and heavy with fruit. The difference between them is the source of spiritual life, grace pouring in! What a sad mistake ever to think that novena devotions are only routine, matter-of-fact, unimportant happenings in one's life! They are the sweeping, surging channels of grace that keep the soul vibrant and tingling and strong.

But we have come a long way from the filling station, haven't we? Call grace what you like. Call it the sap that keeps alive the tree. Or call it the spiritual fuel that helps you up the high hills. It does not matter. Just as long as the supply is never shut off! A perpetual novena is a solid guarantee of heaven's perpetual help.

Queen Mother

The average tourist in Rome is limited to four or five days, perhaps more correctly spelled "daze." But what can you compress into so compact a parenthesis of sight-seeing? Or what will you remember from those hurried and hectic hours when you had the feeling that your brain was a tumbled jumble of bright fragmentary impressions like the rose petals floating in one of those pious paperweights? Curiously, after a dozen years, there still stands out in my memories of the Eternal City, where churches are sprinkled as freely as caraway seeds in rye bread, one comparatively unknown church called St. Mary of the Angels.

What impressed me most was that it did not start out to be a church at all. In the beginning it was a Roman bath, erected under the patronage of the emperor Diocletian. Now, a Roman bath was not the contemporary Hollywood swimming pool, elaborate as some of these may be. It was a whole building, elegant and luxurious, where bathing was brought to the highest plateau of sensuality. This, incidentally, is why some of the early Christian Fathers snorted at the notion that cleanliness was next-door neighbor to godliness. In pagan Rome the cult of cleanliness had fringe nonbenefits of moral corruption.

Anyway, poor Christians, condemned to slavery, sweating under the merciless lash of Roman legionnaires, built these baths of Diocletian. But, as often as they could, they secretly cut into each brick a hairline cross, the symbol of the Christian faith and of Christ. Through the centuries these bricks patiently waited for their master. And the day came when none less than Michelan-

179

gelo drew the plans for a church that would rise on these very ruins and would even use some of these very bricks that were stamped with the sign of the cross. They called the church "St. Mary of the Angels."

All this came back to me when the Roman calendar celebrated the feast of Mary the Queen. For as I knelt before the picture of Our Mother of Perpetual Help, it struck me that this Madonna had worn in anticipation the crown of a queen for almost a hundred years. This crowning of the image had been a papal honor granted because of miracles worked through the intercession of our Lady under that special title of Perpetual Help. The Queenship of Mary was, on the other hand, a very recent feast. But, like the bricks in the Christian church, it seems as though this image of Mary had been quietly expecting this all the time. We at her beloved shrine knew it, and were expecting it, and were ready for it when it came, but instead of a smug, "We told you so," our greeting was a thrilled, "Hail, Holy Queen!"

This feast, mind you, is just a new honor, not a new doctrine. It is only the bursting forth of another blossom on the same bush. Or it is the same tree just wearing the colors of another season. Certainly the words "Mary" and "Queen" are not strangers. After Mass, we older folks used to say, for as far back as we can remember, "Hail, Holy Queen!" In the Litany of Our Lady, where her titles are strung together like glittering stones in a necklace, we invoke her as "Queen of Apostles . . . Queen of Virgins . . . Queen of Martyrs." At Easter time, instead of the Angelus, we say the "Regina Coeli" . . . "Queen of Heaven, rejoice, Alleluia!"

But granted the mellow age of this tradition, what precisely is Mary's right to the title? Is it merely the lyrical enthusiasm of poetic devotion? Far from it! If the Scriptures can salute Mary as, "Blessed are you among women," would not this make her the first and best and therefore Queen of all women? If she alone was preserved immaculate from every smidgeon of sin, free even from that dark and sinister birthmark of every soul called original sin, if she was so unique in her sanctity that even the Protestant poet Wordsworth hails her as "our tainted nature's solitary boast," should she not therefore be the Queen of our race, of all humanity? And above all, if she is the Mother of Christ the King, is she not thereby the Queen of all Christians?

As Queen, Mary does not wear a material crown, but we can easily imagine how such a crown would be studded with rubies of blazing red, because her heart died a martyr's death as she watched her Son, our Savior, bleed slowly to death on the cross; and with pearls of soft white luster to proclaim her purity as Virgin of Virgins; and finally with diamonds for the glistening tears that glided down her cheeks when she lost her Boy for three heartbreaking days near the temple, and later lost the grown Man for three numb days in the tomb.

A queen she is, yes, but not as we envision many of the famous queens of the past, who were haughty and arrogant, high and distant and sniffingly aloof. Mary, after all, remembered when her only kingdom was a hillside cottage, and when one tragic day it was only a hilltop cross. She could never possibly be one of those disdainful princesses who strutted across the stage of history with so much power at their fingertips, fingertips that were long and painted like cruel claws, and with so little pity or virtue in their hearts, and such hearts!

Contrast Mary standing on the shore, waving good-bye to Jesus and the Apostles as their creaking boat raises its forlorn sail — contrast her with Cleopatra, queen of Egypt, as rhythmic banks of dipping oars send her golden barge needling down the Nile. Let the men at those oars strain and pant and die; this cool enameled queen lolls under her silken canopy and does not care. She is the spoiled child of sensual pomp: cynic now, suicide soon, inspiration never.

Or compare Mary with England's first Elizabeth, the queen who turned an island into an empire, queen of the great galleons whose colored sails made rainbows on the seas, and whose captains brought home to her the wealth of the world, pouring it in golden streams at her royal feet. And yet this Elizabeth, this queen during England's triumphant hour, sat stubbornly upon the floor of her bedroom in her last illness, her shaggy red wig askew, and like a pouting child refused to go to her bed till she was carried there by force, trembling and whining. Mary, by contrast, was poor as any housewife, but because she had lived without stain, she faced death without fear. If Death kept his court within the hollow crown of king and queen, he had no terrors for Mary.

How different from her were all those so-called great queens who have swept across the horizon of history, their satin trains trailing behind them, their chins high in the air, their mouths hard and cruel — from Catherine de Medici to Catherine of Russia, all majesty and magnificence and ruthless power, the power that could break any man who opposed them and toss him aside like a peanut shell! Put Mary beside these and hear her whisper to her Son in behalf of an embarrassed country couple, "They have no wine." Or Mary, who confides to her cousin Elizabeth, "My soul proclaims the greatness of the Lord. . . . He has pulled down princes from their thrones and exalted the lowly" (Luke 1:46, 52).

Here is a queen so kind, so considerate, so thoughtful! We count Isabella of Spain a good and generous queen because, as the story has it, she gave some of her jewels so that Columbus might outfit his ships and open to men the new world. But what shall we say of this queen, Mary, who gave her only treasure, the blood-red ruby of the crucified Christ, to pay the ransom that would open to men the kingdom of heaven?

Here then is a queen to be proud of, to pay honor to, to love and to serve! In the dramatic days of chivalry, knights saluted their queen by raising their swords in a steely circle around her, with a pulse-pounding vow to defend her royal person even with their lives. We need not face martyrdom defending the honor of Mary (though history records heroes who have) but we should at least ask ourselves: Just how much does she really mean to us in our daily lives? Is she only an impersonal name in a prayer book, a lifeless statue on a pedestal, a picture on a wall? Do we ever *do* anything just because it will please Mary? Do we ever refrain from doing something because it would, we feel, hurt her or shame us in her eyes? Has Mary any impact on our living? Or is our devotion, our rosaries, our novenas, so much spiritual embroidery, just an ornamental fringe that is not really a part of the fabric of practical life? Is it a kind of pious May-walk for grown-ups?

When we were still preschool youngsters in the Bay Ridge section of Brooklyn, every Saturday in May meant a kind of picnic in the park, only they called it a May-walk. There was a tiny May Queen (sometimes proud, sometimes tearful); there was a Maypole, decorated with colored streamers; there was a ritual by which we were supposed to go skipping around the pole, holding a streamer and singing in thin falsettos the tinkling tunes of childhood. But, let there suddenly sound the call for lunch, or the Good Humor man's ancient ancestor, who rang a handbell and pushed an ice-cream cart, and in mid-syllable the song was over and off we ran, the streamer abruptly snapped off, the bit of crepe paper still in our hand.

Is this possibly the way we act now as adults when the Maypole is really the cross and all the cross stands for, like the Ten Commandments and self-control, loyalty to our Lord and to the Queen of Martyrs who stood beneath that cross? This Queen of the May, Mary, is Virtue and Purity itself. If Temptation beckons with its dainty finger, or if it winks its shifty, lecherous eye, our task is to grip all the more tightly not a paper streamer, but that golden chain that binds a genuine subject of this Queen to her forever.

Holding the line against an insidious and insistent world

is never easy, but in time of temptation we can go to Mary without fear because she is our Mother and therefore has sympathy for our problems, and because she is our Queen and therefore has power to help us.

First Woman of the World

There is a certain swanky prep school in England with a curious blank spot on the wall near the main entrance. Generations of schoolboys have traditionally bowed toward that spot as they passed. Why? They never knew just why. It was a school custom, that was all. But recently some researcher revealed that back in the sixteenth century there had hung on that spot an image of the Madonna. So the boys still go through the motions, but without the proper motive.

It would be a sorry state of affairs if similarly we who honor our Lady would plod the same path of mechanical routine without really adverting to the reasons behind our devotion. Reasons? Rather, reason? Because basically the only reason we honor our Lady is that God has honored her so much more. He did what no mere man could ever do. He chose a certain woman for His Mother, and He chose Mary.

To any thinking individual, Mary has to be tremendously important or utterly insignificant. She was either just another Jewish peasant girl, or she was the Mother of a Son who was divine.

When El Cordobés, the famous Spanish matador, left his native village to make his fortune in the bullring, he embraced his sister in her shabby dress and said, "I will dress you in gold, or I will dress you in black." With him, it was all or nothing. With Mary and ourselves, it has to be the same.

We do not have to roam the earth to discover the status of Mary. It is written, not in the high-flown visions of some mystic, but plainly on the pages of God, the Scriptures, "Blessed are you among women and blessed is the fruit of your womb." "He who shall be born of you shall be called 'Son of the Most High.'"

Because she bore Him in Bethlehem, reared Him in Nazareth, suffered with Him at Calvary, Mary was His Mother, not just in the biological sense, but in the way of the best of mothers with the best of sons. Our Lady was not merely a piece of physical machinery so that the Son of God could be born. She was everything a good mother is, the closest and tenderest and most affectionate woman in a man's life till he takes a wife. But in the blueprint of redemption, our divine Savior had no plans for a wife. Mary was the only woman in His life, and therefore all the dearer to Him.

God esteemed the choice of His Mother so important that He prepared her for that exalted office by the Immaculate Conception. He rewarded her for its fulfillment by assuming her, body and soul, into heaven. Each of these unique distinctions makes excellent sense. The Immaculate Conception (meaning that Mary was preserved from original sin) made certain that Christ would not spring from a tainted source. The Savior of the world must not be like a brook that bubbled from a muddy spring, but must have its beginning in pure mountain snows. Actually the Immaculate Conception was pointed at the glory of Christ, and only secondarily at the sinlessness of Mary. December 8 was really only a remote preparation for December 25.

As to the Assumption, how could God act otherwise? Could He allow the body of Mary, from which He had taken His own sacred flesh, to crumble in the decaying earth and become a banquet for boring worms? Was this the way for God's Mother to end? Because God was almighty, He could bring Mary to Himself, body and soul, as easily as a wealthy man mails his mother an airplane ticket to bring her to his home.

These are the only three doctrines concerning our Lady that the Church has officially proclaimed: namely, that Mary was conceived without sin; that she became the Mother of Jesus, the God-Man; and that she was brought, body and soul, into heaven. Catholics *must* believe these; nothing else about Mary is of a *de fide* obligation.

At the other end of the Marian spectrum there are (we sadly concede) some outlandish exaggerations that make real lovers of our Lady cringe and wince. They shoot out like flamboyant wild flowers from the soil of excessive sentimentality and medieval superstition. This is not faith, it is fanaticism. It is not the rooted position of the official Church; it is the unsteady wanderings of some misled churchgoers. In other words, we Catholics do not adore Mary as a goddess. We do not worship her as divine. We insist that she is only a creature, and as such she can never be even thought of in the same breath as God. In fact, though I say this reluctantly, in the sense that she is a creature, she is infinitely closer to Satan than she can ever be to God. God, as God, has to be on a completely different plane from all creatures, and both Mary and Satan are only creatures.

On the other hand, once you emphasize that Mary is not divine, you cannot exaggerate her position among creatures. Of creatures, Mary is the highest and the first, as the Second Vatican Council solemnly proclaimed, thereby ratifying the Catholic belief held from the earliest ages. Just as the President's wife is the First Lady of the land, God's Mother has to be the First Woman of the world. Silver litanies and gorgeous stained-glass windows, magnificent shrines and majestic basilicas, pale marble statues and glowing Madonnas — these are only the ornamental tassels on that central incredible honor: Mary is the Mother of God.

But if we honor Mary because God chose her to be His Mother, we love her because He left her to us as our Mother too. It was at the crib of Bethlehem without any of the normal pains of childbirth that Mary became the Mother of Jesus. But it was beneath the cross of Calvary, as she agonized by His splintery deathbed, that she became the Mother to us. Now that He was going, Jesus needed her no more, so in that last will whose red seals were His five crimson-crusted wounds, He bequeathed her to us in the proxy of Saint John when He said, "This is your mother."

We need a spiritual mother because problems and trials beset us on every front. There comes to mind out of the dim past a novena preached at St. Anne de Beaupre and a subsequent trip along the Saguenay River. Between picturesque villages with curious names like Tadoussac and Chicoutimi, the river grows dangerously narrow and ominously black, while overhead, hundreds of feet high, there soar up sheer and terrifying, two towering gray peaks. One is Cape Eternity, so called because it looms up straight, unbroken, bleak, awesome. The other is called Cape Trinity, because it seems to rise in three majestic segments.

There is a tale that long ago a fishing ship escaped certain disaster there by invoking the Mother of God. In gratitude, the village placed on the second level of Cape Trinity a huge statue of our Lady. On the day I saw it, the silver sheen of the statue glittered in the sun, and high above it a drifting circle of birds ringed it like a living halo, and Mary, with her folded hands pointed up and her tender face looking down, was the only warm note in a grim and chilling scene.

Instinctively there you looked up to Mary. But should we not often do as much? Are you perhaps at this moment struggling even to survive in this weird land of plenty? Think of our Lady, so poor at Bethlehem that she had to share the roof above her head with stamping beasts, and had to lay her Child in the crackling straw of a feed-trough. Or do you feel that you are discriminated against, frozen out in certain circles, doors quietly shut against you? Mary knew that too. The door of the inn was slammed rattling against her pleading face.

Have you seen cherished dreams come crashing down about you like a crystal chandelier that one moment was all dancing brilliance and the next a clatter of shattering fragments?

187

Mary saw more than a dream come down. She saw her Son — all mangled, bleeding, dead — lowered from the cross. And how unjust it seemed! She had given the world Christmas, and in turn it gave her Good Friday. But she still believed and hoped and prayed, and out of the ruins came the Resurrection!

If we cling to Mary, we shall conquer with Christ!

Beneath the Cross

"Mother of Sorrows" should be a touching title. But phrases are like coins. They may preserve their essential value, but they tend to get worn and thin from use. The first man who talked of the frosting on a cake saw the crusted white glaze of a winter landscape. To us it has long since become a colorless kitchen cliché. (We even have pink frosting! Sunset on the Alps or the Rockies?)

"Mother of Sorrows" too — because the tragedy happened so long ago, and because it is all embalmed in the nice smooth amber of history — can become just a dull, dead scrap of pious language with no ringing impact on our minds. It would be a pity for us and a crime against her if we thought of Mary only as a pale carved statue, a static figure in a conventional Calvary group.

When Mary stood at the foot of the cross, her swimming eyes were probably on a level with the pierced feet of her dying Son. If she wanted to see His face, she had to tilt her head and look up. And when she saw that face, it must have been one great scarlet smear. The sharp brown thorns jutted out around a face that drooped like a tattered red rose.

When Mary looked up at the dark brown tower of the cross, did it poignantly remind her in reverse of His tiny baby days when, as the poet says, "He climbed the Ivory Tower of her body and kissed the Mystical Rose upon her lips"? Or did her mother's memory play her tricks and make her see Him when He was a lad up in a neighborhood cherry tree and offering her some cherries from a hand that was stained crimson? Now He is up there on that grim tree of the cross, and His hands hold only the blood-smeared heads of iron spikes.

Oh, the agony as she looked up! And, oh, the anguish as He looked down!

Right after the First World War they gave a reception in a grand New York hotel to America's aviation ace, Captain Eddie Rickenbacker. Crystal glittered, flowers glowed, uniforms blazed, gowns and jewels gleamed and sparkled in the swankiest of settings. Toasts were ceremoniously proposed. "To the President!" "To the flag!" "To the Lafayette Escadrille!"

Finally they asked the guest of honor to propose his toast. He looked along the head table with its dazzle of dignitaries, out across the vast ballroom with its cream of society and its wealthy tycoons. Then his eyes slowly wandered to the balcony. They swept along till they stopped at an unassuming little woman in black. He looked at her for one intense moment. Then young Rickenbacker squared his shoulders, clicked his heels, raised his glass and all but shouted, "To my mother!"

In an instant every person in that hall was on his feet. They cheered her and him till the blinking chandeliers all but swayed.

At Calvary the blood-rimmed eyes of Jesus looked *down*, swept along the motley crowd beneath the cross, past soldiers and Pharisees and curious spectators, and there, at the very foot of the cross His gaze fixed on Mary, His Mother. At a wedding the father gives away the daughter. At this deathbed the Son gave away the Mother. That day when He had given His body to the cross, His garments to the executioners, His forgiveness to His enemies, Paradise to the Good Thief, now in a last will whose red seal was His blood-crusted wounds, He gave away His Mother. Gave her to us by the proxy of Saint John.

As she stood there by the upright brown beam of the cross

that stood like a grandfather's clock whose *tick, tick* was the *drip, drip* of blood, and whose Victim's motionless but divine hands told not time but eternity, was she not truly the Queen of Martyrs? Not into her hands or into her side plunged spear or nails, but into her heart!

I have seen a church in New York City where statues of martyrs, carved in wood and tinted with vivid colors, stand upon pedestals high along the walls. Each martyr there symbolically holds in his hands a small replica of the weapon that finished him off. Thus Saint Paul holds the sword that beheaded him, Saint Matthew the club that felled him, Saint Lawrence the gridiron that roasted him, Saint Andrew that strange cross, shaped like an X, on which they stretched him out to die.

In a tiny side chapel of that church there is a statue of Mary, the Queen of Martyrs. But if Mary is the Queen of Martyrs, what was the instrument of her martyrdom? What does she hold in *her* hands? Very pointedly the statue there, somewhat like the "Pietà" of Michelangelo, shows Mary seated and holding the dead body of Christ. This was the instrument of her torture! It was the sufferings of Christ that made Mary the Queen of Martyrs. Every blow of the hammer rang against her heart. Each nail pierced her soul. Every thorn pushed its cruel needle into her brain. Just to see Him suffer and die on that darkling hill while the curious mob drank in the spectacle like a bloody Roman circus was martyrdom itself.

Suppose our road home today — or tomorrow — took us over the bare brow of Calvary's hill, and we suddenly came upon Mary standing at the foot of the cross. And suppose she said with that dazed, distant look of the suddenly bereaved, "Why did this have to happen?" Would we answer that there was greed in the itching, greedy palms of Judas, or that there was cowardice in the lily-white, water-sloshed hands of Pilate, or that there was hatred in the clenched hands of the high priests and the mob — and that was why the hands of Jesus burned with the red fire of bleeding wounds? True enough, but really these were only the shallow surface reasons behind the Crucifixion of Christ. Deep down, the reasons were the sins of us all. Saint Paul got to the heart of the matter when he said: "He loved me, and he gave himself up for me."

But in the process Mary suffered too. There at the foot of the cross, longing to push the blood-matted hair away from His eyes, longing to bathe His face with a cool moist cloth, longing to do something, anything — was not Mary there a symbol of all those who stand so helplessly at the foot of a hospital deathbed, feeling futile and frustrated and perhaps in deeper agony than the sedated patient?

To the mother who sits beside a coffin in the artificial garden of the funeral home, with its pillows of roses and crosses of lilies and the pink ribbons and the gilt letters, or to the mother who dreams of one white cross in a regiment of white crosses in some distant spot that she never heard of till her boy died there . . . Tulagi, Guadalcanal, Iwo Jima, Korea, Vietnam . . . to every mother of sorrow the arms of Mary go out in sympathy and comfort, because she in an even crueler way knew the red shock of tragedy and the aching black emptiness of loss.

With sinners, too, the sorrowful Mary has a strange kinship because in her own vivid way she knew what it was like to lose God. When they left His ashen corpse in the tomb, and she dragged herself back to some relative's house, it was like going into another tomb. The house seemed vacant, the walls were blank, the very silence ached. For the first time He was really gone out of her life, and her heart was a bleak desert of numbing loneliness, her soul a spiritual vacuum. Good Friday for us is just a pale hint of how it was with her — when we look up at the bare altar and the empty tabernacle with its door so strangely ajar. God is gone, and the most elegant church is only an empty hall. It was perhaps during those few fearful days, the first Good Friday and Holy Saturday, that Mary learned to be the Refuge of Sinners, to pity those who had lost God and to guide them back to His presence and His grace.

On some shoulders God lays crosses so heavy we wonder how they bear up. This thought comes to me as I glance across the desk and my eye falls on a ceramic ashtray. It so happens that I have not smoked for many years, but this ashtray I would not easily surrender. It was painted by a girl of twenty-one who not long ago was in a tragic automobile accident. She is paralyzed from the neck down. She painted that ashtray with a wisp of a paintbrush gripped in her teeth.

She makes me reflect on two facts. One, how little most of us really have to suffer, with our matchstick crosses, our thumb-tack crucifixions, our crepe-paper Calvaries. Secondly, how much superhuman (supernatural is the better word) courage God can still send to us through the channel of His Mother, when we have (as this smiling girl does) a deep devotion to her. Her sorrows can be the source of our strength. She who stood by the foot of the cross can still stand by us. Our Lady of the Broken Heart earned the gift of soothing the hearts of all.